VIRGINIA

AND THE

FRENCH AND INDIAN WAR

Hayes Baker-Crothers, Ph.D.

Professor of History, University of Maryland

HERITAGE BOOKS
2007

HERITAGE BOOKS
AN IMPRINT OF HERITAGE BOOKS, INC.

Books, CDs, and more—Worldwide

For our listing of thousands of titles see our website
at
www.HeritageBooks.com

A Facsimile Reprint
Published 2007 by
HERITAGE BOOKS, INC.
Publishing Division
65 East Main Street
Westminster, Maryland 21157-5026

Copyright © 1928 University of Chicago

Composed and Printed by
The University fo Chicago Press
Chicago, Illinois
May 1928

International Standard Book Number: 978-0-7884-1004-0

TO MY WIFE
RUTH ALLISON HUDNUT

THE UNIVERSITY OF CHICAGO PRESS
CHICAGO, ILLINOIS

THE BAKER & TAYLOR COMPANY
NEW YORK

THE MACMILLAN COMPANY OF CANADA, LIMITED
TORONTO

THE CAMBRIDGE UNIVERSITY PRESS
LONDON

THE MARUZEN-KABUSHIKI-KAISHA
TOKYO, OSAKA, KYOTO, FUKUOKA, SENDAI

THE COMMERCIAL PRESS, LIMITED
SHANGHAI

PREFACE

This study is preliminary to a larger work which will accomplish for each of the colonies what I hope to have accomplished for Virginia. While much has been written regarding the relations between the mother-country and the colonies during this period, it has been from the point of view of Great Britain rather than that of the colonies. This study, as its title indicates, seeks to describe and explain the reaction of the *people* of Virginia toward the French and Indian War. As that reaction was probably affected by the colonies in close proximity to Virginia and grouped with her for war purposes, minor consideration has also been given to the provinces of Pennsylvania, Maryland, North and South Carolina.

In determining the attitude of any people toward any stimulus an understanding of the reasons for that attitude is essential, and I have thus been led to an investigation into the life of the people from an economic, social, and political aspect. Throughout I have tried to divest myself of those influences which would make me view my subject from the standpoint of present-day conditions, to surround myself with the atmosphere of the ordinary man living in that period, and to remember that such an individual could not understand the importance of the interior nor foresee the decisive nature of the conflict. While some few leaders, better informed and more imaginative than the general population, realized the great issues at stake, the Babbit of yesterday, like the

Babbit of today, was limited by the narrow horizon of his everyday life and interested only in events touching his immediate experience.

The sources which form the basis of this work will be found in the bibliographical note.

I desire to express my gratitude to Professor W. T. Root, for encouragement, advice, and constructive criticism in all stages of the work, and to my wife, Ruth Allison Hudnut, for valued assistance.

HAYES BAKER-CROTHERS

CONTENTS

CHAPTER I

THE UNDERLYING CAUSE OF THE FRENCH AND INDIAN WAR

In order to secure an adequate understanding of the attitude of Virginia toward the French and Indian War it is necessary to consider briefly the general reasons for the Anglo-French conflicts in the eighteenth century. The immediate cause of the struggle between England and France lay in their economic policies. Both were animated by the ideal of a self-sufficient state that should be largely independent of outside nations, and to that end were attempting to build colonial empires.

A realization of the English ideal demanded commercial expansion. Measures for the advancement of trade were initiated by private individuals and were followed up and protected by the state on demand of the investors as essential to the interests of the nation. The French worked toward the same end, but, dominated by paternalism, the state made the first advances and carried business with it into new fields of endeavor. From the ambition of the two nations to establish this ideal resulted their conflicts, essentially commercial in character, conducted in the interests of the mercantile classes which stood in close alliance with the government.

In North America the particular objects of controversy were control of the fisheries, land, and the Indian trade. From 1690 to 1763 Great Britain engaged in four struggles with her great rival, France, for the trade and dominion of the New World. The treaties of Ryswick, Utrecht, and Aix la Chapelle, closing the first three conflicts, brought no solution of the important issues at stake in North America, of which the most outstanding in the middle of the century was the domination of the trans-Allegheny West. This was the dominant cause of the French and Indian War.

Immediately giving rise to the contest for the West was the clash between the nationals of the two rivals over the Indian trade. The early colonial records are replete with evidences of its importance.[1] In a short time the fur-trade country near the coast became exhausted, and trade shifted to the West. British traders appeared in this region early in the eighteenth century. Conrad Weiser, an Indian agent chiefly in the employ of Pennsylvania, reported in 1754 to the commissioners at Albany that Pennsylvania traders had been going to the Allegheny for over 30 years.[2] Not only had Pennsylvania traders been for years in the backlands, but also those from New York and from as far south as the Carolinas.[3]

The colonies with direct access to the Great Lakes and the Mississippi Valley acquired a virtual monopoly

[1] C. H. McIlwain, editor, *Wraxall's Abridgement of the New York Indian Records, 1678–1751,* pp. xxviii–xxxiv.

[2] E. B. O'Callaghan, editor, *Documents Relative to the Colonial History of the State of New York,* VI, 872.

[3] R. G. Thwaites, editor, *Collections of the State Historical Society of Wisconsin,* XVI, 303, 325, 331, 345; *New York Colonial Documents,* IX, 953.

of the British trade.[4] Water routes to the lake country gave New York an advantage in that region denied the central and southern colonies by the mountain barriers along their frontiers. Pennsylvania and Virginia both suffered from this handicap. Pennsylvania, with no outlet to the north and with Virginia in possession of the easy valley route to the south, had approach only to the western fur trading area. This was open to her by mountain passes. With a practical monopoly of these passes, Pennsylvania traders, tireless in their efforts, soon dominated the Indian trade of the Ohio region.[5] Virginia traders, while crossing the Alleghanies to the Ohio country at an early date, did not build up a large trade in the West. They took the road of least resistance and went south along the valley route to the backlands of the Carolinas, where they traded with the Cherokees.[6] The southermost colonies, with their Indian trade chiefly in their own hinterland, sent but few traders into the Ohio region where they came in contact with the French.[7]

In the ten years before 1750 British traders made their way into almost every Indian village in the Ohio district. George Croghan and others of Pennsylvania had stores on Lake Erie, the Ohio River, and in the country of the Miami, Scioto, and Muskingum rivers. Croghan was the prince of Pennsylvania traders and carried on a flourishing trade with the Twightwees or Miamis of the Wabash and Miami rivers.[8] By 1750

---

[4] *Wraxall's Abridgement*, p. xv.

[5] C. A. Hanna, *The Wilderness Trail*, I, 2, 3, 6, 22.

[6] *Wraxall's Abridgement*, p. xxxiii. [7] *Ibid.*, pp. xxxiii–xxxiv.

[8] Hanna, *Wilderness Trail*, I, xxiii, 3, 6, 17, 175; II, 12.

trading posts were established at the Indian towns
of Loggstown, Kuskies, Muskingum, Lower Shawnee
Town, Alleghany, and old Shawnee Town.[9] British traders were erecting houses at Sandusky Bay in 1754.[10] In
1748 Pickawillany, on the Big Miami, was founded.[11]
Three years later Christopher Gist, an Indian trader of
the better type working for the Ohio Company, found
fifty British traders gathered there.[12] It was estimated
in 1748 that during a single season three hundred British
traders made their way into the Ohio valley.[13]

Great numbers of traders were going to the Indians
with British goods to barter for furs. Furs to the extent
of £90,000 sterling, it was estimated, were exported
yearly to England, and a like amount was used in the
colonies.[14] New France sent the same raw product to the
value of £135,000 sterling annually to the mother-country.[15] In return for furs, British traders gave guns, pow-
der, bar lead, duffels, knives, flints, shirts, gartering,
vermillion, looking-glasses, brass kettles, hatchets, rings,
medals and blades, ribbon, dutch pipes, jointed babies,

[9] Located respectively in the present-day counties of Beaver, Lawrence, Coshocton, Scioto, Alleghany.

[10] Dr. John Mitchell's map, cited in Hanna, *Wilderness Trail*, I,
21; Hanna, *Wilderness Trail*, I, 322.

[11] Hanna, *Wilderness Trail*, I, 322.

[12] W. M. Darlington, editor, *Journals of Christopher Gist*, pp. 44–
45.

[13] J. Winsor, *The Mississippi Basin*, p. 249.

[14] "Observations on the Late and Present Conduct of the French
with Regard to Their Encroachments upon the British Colonies in
North America," *Magazine of History*, Extra Numbers, XVI, 12.

[15] *Ibid.*, p. 125.

hats, shoes, tin pots, stockings, hoes, scissors, combs, needles, rum, half-thicks, jew's-harps, etc.—all goods of British manufacture.[16] The Indian trade thus fitted directly into the British mercantile system. Raw products, not competing with those of Great Britain, were received from the West, and a market created there for British wares.

A trade fitting so perfectly into the British economic system of that day was in time bound to receive support from the government. Before King George's War, 1744–48, the government had not worked out an Indian policy; the colonies were given a free hand in the solution of western problems. During that struggle, however, the Crown evidently was awakened to the danger of the French closing the routes through the Alleghanies to the west and obstructing the Indian trade, now of growing importance. Halifax, president of the Board of Trade, supported by Bedford, secretary of st te, favored the formation of the Ohio Company in 1749 as a means to block the French advance and to encourage the British Indian trade.[17] The company, composed of prominent Virginians and British financiers, sought to profit from the fur trade and land speculation. Thomas Lee, a member of the company and president of the Virginia council, claimed that the company's grant of 2,000,000 acres on the upper Ohio was to protect Virginia's fur trade, the trade of neighboring colonies, and to furnish goods to the

[16] Lists of presents to Indians, Hanna, *Wilderness Trail*, II, 316–18.

[17] *Journals of the Board of Trade*, LVII, 1749; Alvord, *The Mississippi Valley in British Politics*, I, 87; C. O. 5. 1347, additional instruction to William Gooch, December 13, 1748.

Indians, who then need have no further dealings with the French. The condition placed on the grant by the Crown was the building of a fort and the locating of families to make a strong settlement on Virginia's frontier.[18]

The Ohio Company received its charter because the home government was sensitive to commercial interests and because the company's objects coincided with the aims of the ministry to further Indian trade and to stop French occupation of the Ohio.

While the Crown at this time was unwilling to form a definite western policy, different views on western problems were developing both in the colonies and in England.[19] In the colonies the conflict of opinion centered chiefly on whether colonial or imperial rights to land west of the Alleghanies should dominate. Those persons who desired that each province develop its own western land claims stressed charter rights. Their chief strength lay in the colonies possessing western lands: Virginia, Massachusetts, Connecticut, New York, the Carolinas, and Georgia. Virginia in particular had vast western claims, and individuals in that colony were ready to take advantage of the territorial pretensions of the province which dated back to its charter of 1609. These persons united with British financial interests in the Ohio Company or combined in such local speculative or-

[18] *Minutes of the Provincial Council of Pennsylvania, 1683–1776,* V, 423. Referred to hereafter as *Pa. Col. Recs.*

[19] Alvord, *Mississippi Valley in British Politics,* I, 105–7; *The Advantages of the Definitive Treaty,* 27, cited in G. L. Beer, *British Colonial Policy 1754–65,* pp. 132–59.

ganizations as the Loyal and Greenbriar companies with the aim of exploiting the West.[20]

This monopoly of the West by a few colonies was opposed by the other colonial faction which emphasized imperial rights in the land and advocated Crown control of the West. When the party acquired strength it favored the formation of new colonies in the West and upheld the advantages accruing from the enrichment of the British treasury by the judicious sale of western land. Although its principal strength was in the colonies, its ideal inspired patriotism and won adherents in England as well. In the colonies its chief advocates were the provinces having definite western boundaries, particularly Pennsylvania and Maryland, where the desire to participate in the benefits of western land was accentuated by the fear that Virginia's power might become overgreat if she was allowed to exploit her western claims.[21]

In England the main controversy over trans-Alleghany problems arose from a difference of viewpoint based on an economic principle. The older theory considered the chief purpose of colonies was the production of raw goods which could be carried to the mother-country in British ships. The newer idea maintained that colonies would be more valuable as markets for the disposal of British goods. The advocates of the older idea wished to maintain and encourage the western fur trade

[20] Alvord, *Mississippi Valley in British Politics*, I, 106–10; lists of land grants in *Virginia Magazine of History and Biography*, V, 175 ff., 241 ff.

[21] Alvord, *Mississippi Valley in British Politics*, I, 110–11; A. H. Smyth, editor, *Benjamin Franklin's Writings*, III, 206, 358.

which was dependent upon primitive conditions. They therefore opposed expansion to the West and its settlement.[22] The adherents of the newer theory believed that the value of colonies as markets would be enhanced by an increase both in the number and population of colonies. At the same time they favored keeping the colonies as agricultural communities so that their products would not compete with those of the mother-country, and advocated the opening up and settlement of the West.[23] While these parties were strong in England, at no time in the earlier period were they able to force their will on the ministry, which would go no farther in determining western policy than to give consent to the Ohio Company's charter.

The indications of the Crown's greater interest in the West, revealed by the grant to the Ohio Company, produced a change in the attitude of the governors of Pennsylvania and Virginia toward the Ohio Indian trade. The treaty of Lancaster, 1744, contained faint signs of co-operation by the two colonies,[24] but to 1748 there was practically no official support of the Indian trade by the governors of the colonies. This was the logical result of the absence of any Indian policy by the Crown. With the slight encouragement which the governors received when the Crown permitted the formation

[22] Alvord, *Mississippi Valley in British Politics*, I, 107–8; *Wraxall's Abridgement*, chaps. i–ii.

[23] Beer, *British Colonial Policy*, pp. 132–39; Alvord, *Mississippi Valley in British Politics*, I, 108–9.

[24] *Virginia Magazine of History and Biography*, XIII, 160–61; R. A. Brock, editor, *The Official Records of Robert Dinwiddie, 1751–58*, I, 6 n.

of the Ohio Company, their attitude became more aggressive.' Possibly they recognized the reasons which actuated Great Britain, and being in close touch with the situation, saw more clearly that a clash was inevitable. This naturally made them take a course slightly in advance of the Crown. They were sensitive to the developments of British policy toward the West and were ready to seize upon any pretext to forestall the French and advance the trade and land interests of their own colonies. Their measures were treaties, conferences, messengers, and gifts to the Indians, activities intended to win them from the French and attach them firmly to English interests. But their success was limited by failure to make a common cause and by concentration on the advantages to be gained for a particular colony rather than for the British possessions in North America as a whole. This resulted in duplication and contradiction of effort, in separate conferences with the Indians, the independent sending of messengers and gifts.[25]

Robert Dinwiddie, as governor of Virginia and a member of the Ohio Company, naturally had a special interest in forwarding its fortunes. He knew the company was favored as a means of thwarting the designs of the French in the West, and he could hardly afford to lose the opportunity of benefiting the colony by securing for it a good share of the Ohio Indian trade then monopolized by Pennsylvania traders. He also probably realized that actual possession by the Ohio Company of a

[25] *Pa. Col. Recs.*, V, 316–18, 347–58, 423, 434, 438, 450–51, 463, 467, 485, 487, 517–18, 519–24, 657–59, 712–13.

grant of land in an area in dispute between the colonies would strengthen the claims of Virginia.

Governor Hamilton of Pennsylvania likewise had a keen concern in the fortunes of this company, for he knew one of its objects was trade and its success meant a sharing of Pennsylvania's monopoly with Virginia. He was still more agitated by the company's land grant, which affected in no small degree the interest of the Penn family in the land.[26] Although the Loggstown Conference of 1752 with the Indians was held primarily for the benefit of the Ohio Company,[27] Hamilton participated in it, probably influenced by a desire to keep a check on Virginia's activities. Dinwiddie, also moved by colonial particularism, instructed his commissioners to select interpreters devoted to the Indian trade of Virginia and not too much attached to that of her rival.[28] The incident illustrates the conflicting interests of the governors which influenced their conduct toward the Indians and limited English success in the West.

The conference was successful in clearing the Indian title to the land. The cession of territory to the Ohio made at Lancaster, 1744, was confirmed, information of French activities elicited, the right to build at the Ohio forks obtained, permission secured to make a settlement around the fort, and the Indians assured that the company's chief object was trade and friendship with them.[29] The company was now free to push its project vigorously. A factory already established at Wills Creek,

---

[26] *Ibid.*, V, 629–30.   [27] *Journals of Christopher Gist, passim.*
[28] *Virginia Magazine of History and Biography*, XIII, 149–50.
[29] *Ibid.*, pp. 155–74.

a branch of the upper Potomac, was not well located to facilitate trade because it was too far east to attract buyers.[30] Therefore it was necessary to make a better road across the mountains. Gist and Thomas Cresap, one of the directors of the company, with a body of Indians constructed a trail from Wills Creek to Redstone Old Fort on the Monongahela, a distance of about 80 miles over the Alleghany divide, 3,000 feet high.[31] The company's next move was to prepare for the erection of two forts, as required in terms of an additional land grant given in answer to its second petition made in 1752.[32] Its resolve was probably strengthened by rumors of French intentions to occupy the Presque Isle-Allegheny route. To forestall the French, William Trent was sent to select a place for a fort at the forks of the Ohio.[33]

The Ohio Company's moves were supported by Dinwiddie, who, in addition to aiding the company, also attempted to advance general interests by reconciling the northern and southern Indians, allies of the English, but constantly at war with each other. He sent Colonel William Fairfax in 1753 as a representative of Virginia to meet the chiefs of the Iroquois at Winchester, give them presents, and arrange for another conference at the same place in 1754 to which representatives of the southern nations would be invited.[34] Dinwiddie expected to rec-

[30] H. T. Leyland, "The Ohio Company," *Quarterly Publication of the Historical and Philosophical Society of Ohio*, XVI, 13-14.

[31] Hanna, *Wilderness Trail*, I, 105.

[32] *Journals of Christopher Gist*, p. 237.

[33] *Pa. Col. Recs.*, V, 659-60.   [34] *Ibid.*, V, 657, 688, 709, 713.

oncile the differences between these hereditary enemies at this meeting. If at the same time he could hold the Ohio Indians by trade interests, he could attain his aim and present a solid front to the French along the whole western frontier.

Dinwiddie's active policy in the West received the cautious support of the Board of Trade. Letters from the Board to Dinwiddie show no attempt on its part to manage Indian affairs, but rather to continue the old policy of giving each colony a free hand. The Board commended Dinwiddie's practice of giving presents to the Indians, and advised fairness in all dealings with them.[35] The support of Indians, such as the Miamis, at war with the French, was recommended. The question of French aggressions was turned over to the secretary of state. Dinwiddie's other projects, for instance, the building of small forts on the Ohio waters, were approved, and cannon which he had requested were sent him. In general, the Board favored Dinwiddie's measures for the Ohio Company, his Indian policy, and his general scheme of forwarding British interests in the West. The Board's approval was based on its desire to maintain the British position and trade in the hinterland and its belief that the best way to do this, aside from conquest, was to build up alliances with the Indians.[36]

But the French were becoming alarmed by British trading activities, and by the fourth decade of the cen-

[35] C. O. 5. 1366, letter of B.T. to Governor Dinwiddie, November 29, 1752.

[36] C. O. 5. 1367, letter of B.T. to Governor Dinwiddie, January 17, June 6, 1753.

tury realized that they constituted a real menace. De Noyan, at Detroit, wrote in 1741: "The English have been coming For a Number of Years to corrupt the Savages Within the Sphere of this Post and I have resolved to have them pillaged."[37] The increasing activity of British traders whose continued incursions into the West won away the Indians and their prized furs was threatening French supremacy, and the French resolved to block the English advance.

The Indian trade was the foundation of the prosperity and very existence of New France. It was supported and protected by a government which sought to maintain friendly relations with the Indians by drawing them into close alliance. The alliances once formed not only served as a basis for friendship, but pledged the Indians to hostility to the British though the two white nations might be at peace. Trade was the motive for all Indian treaties. Their continuance and stability were dependent primarily on this factor, which formed the basis for all Indian relations, whether British or French.[38]

The French government controlled not only the trade acquired in this way, but also the people engaged in it, by farming the industry to the highest bidder. Traders were limited in their operations to posts established by the Crown to extend and unify the possible trading areas. France aimed at a monopoly; and although she dominated the two centers of trade, Quebec and New Orleans in the St. Lawrence and Mississippi basins, they were useless unless she controlled the routes

[37] *Wisconsin Historical Collection*, XVII, 358.
[38] *Wraxall's Abridgement*, p. xl.

connecting the fur-trading regions with the centers. Her advance from Quebec soon established Fort Frontenac on Lake Ontario, Forts Niagara, Detroit, Michilimackinac, and Fort Ste Marie, thus giving her control of the Great Lakes. Only on Ontario, where the British had established Oswego, an outpost in their trade with the Six Nations, was her domination of this route contested. Communication south from the Great Lakes through the Ohio country to the Mississippi could be secured by two good routes. The first extended from the western end of Lake Erie by the Maumee River and then by portage to either the Wabash or Miami rivers, tributaries of the Ohio; the second, from the eastern end of the lake by way of Presque Isle[39] and the Allegheny River.

The French became acquainted with the Maumee-Wabash-Miami route first because their search for the richest fur country led them westward through the Great Lakes past the territory surrounding the eastern end of Lake Erie, where the fur country was less valuable and was controlled by the Iroquois, whose hostility made occupation difficult. For these reasons the longer route to the West became their principal means of entry to the Ohio trading country and of communication with the posts on the Mississippi. To control this passage more completely the French established armed posts at points on the Maumee-Wabash route, but neglected to guard the Miami branch. British traders took advantage of this situation when they set up the trading post at Pickawillany which not only blocked the Miami route and

[39] Presque Isle not established at this time.

menaced the Wabash, but also lessened French influence with the Indians.

The second route at the eastern end of Lake Erie, at first neglected for the safer and more familiar but less direct way leading from the western end of the lake, became of special interest to the French because of the increasing trading activities of the British. By taking possession of this route the French would not only secure the shortest road from Quebec to the Mississippi, but also establish themselves in the hinterland of Pennsylvania and Virginia. This position would place them directly across the routes followed by the Pennsylvania and Virginia traders on their way to the Ohio Indians, and would enable the French to prevent direct encroachment on their trade south of the Great Lakes.

Three moves were necessary if the French were to obtain the monopoly of the fur trade in the West: the closing of the trade door through New York, the destruction of Pickawillany, and the possession of the Presque Isle-Allegheny route. The traffic lines through central New York were controlled by the Iroquois, who were friendly to the nation holding Albany: first the Dutch, then the English. This friendship was due in part to the lower prices at which the British sold their goods, but more especially to the peculiar geographical position of the Iroquois. The Six Nations, located in central New York between the white settlements and the West, enjoyed the rôle of middlemen in the fur trade between the far-western Indians and the British. As the fur possibilities of New York were exhausted at an early date, trade interests made the Iroquois attempt to extend their power over the Indians to the West, and they gained a dominating influence over the tribes as far west as the Mississippi. The position held by the Iroquois with the British could not be maintained with the French because France reached the direct field of trade by her own posts on the Great Lakes. Then, too, although the Iroquois defeated the Canadian Indians, they could not force them to bring their furs to New York. Trade thus determined the Iroquois alliances and friendship with the British, while the knowledge of the advantages of the middleman position and their desire to keep it made them hostile to direct trading by the British with the western Indians. This probably accounts for Oswego being the British trading post farthest west and the strategic point of Niagara being left unguarded.[40]

Oswego was a thorn in the side of the French, for it menaced French communication west by contesting their control of the Great Lakes. Its destruction was vital to the French, who sought to weaken the British hold on the lakes. Governor Jonquiere intrusted the task of stirring up the Iroquois against the British post at Oswego to Piquet, the Jesuit father at La Presentation. All through the period from 1748 to 1754 French priests attempted to make converts of the Iroquois and to weaken the influence of the British with them.[41] The French continually encouraged the Iroquois to make war on the southern Indians[42] in the hope that the British would be drawn into the conflict, their friendship with the Iro-

[40] *Wraxall's Abridgement*, pp. xl–xlv.

[41] Winsor, *Mississippi Basin*, pp. 225, 228, 286–87.

[42] *New York Colonial Documents*, VI, 546–47, 588, 742.

quois weakened, and their operations on the Ohio broken up. The method followed was intrigue, but it had no success. Trade interests held the Iroquois firmly to their British alliance. The second move made by the French was the taking of Pickawillany. In 1752 Charles Langlade, with a force of French and Indians, destroyed this trading post and severely punished the Miamis, the Indian allies of the British. Langlade's success opened the Miami route, removed the British threat to the Maumee-Wabash route, and materially lessened British influence with the Ohio Indians.

The destruction of Pickawillany was the first resort to violence by an official French force, and probably strengthened the French determination to gain their third objective, control of the Ohio region near the Alleghanies. As early as 1749 Galissonnière, the French governor, had sent Céléron de Bienville to take possession of the Ohio points, to discover the temper of the Indians, and to drive out the British traders. Céléron made the trip, buried his lead plates setting forth the French title to the region, and took formal possession of the country. He found the Indians friendly to the British and hostile to the French because of lower-priced goods of the British traders. These traders were warned to leave and given messages to the English governors asking them to prevent such trespasses in the future or the traders would be driven out by force.[43] Céléron's warnings had no deterring effect upon the British, and in 1752 the French established armed posts at Presque Isle

[43] Hanna, *Wilderness Trail*, II, 262–64.

and farther south at Le Boeuf on French Creek and at Fort Venango, where French Creek joined the Allegheny.

The British learned of these moves when Colonel Trent, who had been at the forks of the Ohio to select a place for the Ohio Company's fort, brought back the news to Dinwiddie. That official and the other colonial governors in August, 1753, had received instructions from the Earl of Holdernesse, secretary of state, dealing with the invasion of British soil by the French. These instructions commanded the governors to obtain the withdrawal of the encroaching French and Indians by warnings, and, if peaceable means failed, to employ force. The governors were enjoined not to use violence unless they were positive that the undoubted limits of British territory had been invaded, for the two nations were officially at peace.[44] This injunction was doubtless prompted by a desire to refrain from placing England in the position of an aggressor in time of peace.[45] In compliance with these instructions Dinwiddie sent Washington to the Ohio with a formal demand for the withdrawal of the French forces. At the same time he was to secure indubitable evidence of the French intentions. Washington received an answer that left no doubt of the French determination to remain in the upper Ohio region, and so reported to Dinwiddie.[46]

[44] *Pa. Col. Recs.*, V, 689–90; *New York Colonial Documents*, VI, 794–95.

[45] W. T. Root, *The Relations of Pennsylvania with the British Government, 1696–1765*, p. 295.

[46] *Pa. Col. Recs.*, V, 714.

. Washington's report convinced Dinwiddie that there was no recourse but war. The intention of the French to advance south to the "forks," and to fortify that strategic point for the purpose of controlling the upper Ohio territory was evident. On Dinwiddie would fall the task of blocking it, and he knew that as governor of a colony with claims to great western territories on which the French were encroaching, the home government would expect him to support colonial as well as imperial interests. For these reasons at the opening of 1754 he sent Colonel Trent to the Ohio to begin the erection of a fort at the "forks," and issued a proclamation promising to grant 200,000 acres of land near the Ohio forks to be divided among the men volunteering for service against the French.[47] During the early spring Dinwiddie assembled and organized a little army of Virginians which, under the command of Colonel Frye, moved toward the Ohio. A call for reinforcements from Trent because of threats from the French sent Washington ahead with aid. While he was advancing, the French drove off Trent's party, marched down upon Washington's, and captured it. This left the Ohio territory and its trade routes in French possession. A state of actual war existed on the western frontiers of the central and southern colonies.

Hostilities were brought on by the economic policies of England and France. Both adhered to closed trade, refusing foreign nationals a part in Indian trade, though both countries had expressly conceded each other's right to share in such trade in the Treaty of Utrecht.[48] The

[47] *Ibid.*, V, 766–67.   [48] Winsor, *Mississippi Basin*, p. 332.

French, by placing individual traders at armed posts, made trade a part of government policy. England permitted its citizens to make private ventures and then backed them by force of arms, likewise making trade a part of government policy. Either system, under the dominant mercantile theories of the day, precluded peaceful competition by a rival nation. France was in the fur-trade region first, and for a time was able to monopolize it. From the very beginning she resented British intrusion into the west.[49] When competition became keen and her monopoly began to break down before the growing influence of the British with the Indians south of the Great Lakes she considered that the very life of New France was threatened. Her defense was the forcible expulsion of her competitors and an attempt to control the trade routes leading to the fur country by the establishment of armed posts at strategic points.

Unfortunately for French success, the British found the fur trade profitable and were in the West in large numbers. The trade was valuable enough to warrant support. Colonial governors upheld by the home government sent messengers to the Indians, made alliances binding them to the British and pledging them to hostility to the French. The British, like the French, refused to brook rivalry in the Indian trade.

In the early stages of this struggle for trade, when both nations were supporting their traders, the land, except as a means of controlling the lines of commerce, played a relatively small part. While there was land hunger among the colonists, there was still territory east

[49] *Ibid.*

of the Appalachians sufficient for all needs. The actual advance over the mountains by home seekers had not begun as late as 1754. Land settlement had hardly reached the Alleghanies, while British trade with the Indians had spread over the whole region south of the Great Lakes and raised the question of who should control.[50] This could be answered in but one way by countries animated by narrow economic ideas and imperialistic ambitions which made them willing to use force in support of Indian trade and claims to western territory.

[50] C. O. 5. 1273, letter of Governor Hamilton to B.T., February 8, 1750.

CHAPTER II

COLONIAL INACTION

During the period of hostilities prior to the official declaration of war by England and France, Virginia occupied a more prominent position than did the other colonies. The conflict was centered in territory which Virginia claimed by charter. Pennsylvania had claims to parts of the same area, but had no company similar to the Ohio Company, composed largely of her citizens, to give strength to her claims by a definite grant of land in the disputed region. Pennsylvania was a proprietary colony whose governor was more dependent on the proprietor than on the Crown for his position, and for this reason had less incentive to carry out Crown policies. The Quaker ruling class and German Pietists through religious principles were opposed to war. It is not strange, therefore, that Virginia was more alert to the French threat. Her claims to the contested area were greater. Dinwiddie was directly responsible to the Crown; he was personally interested in a commercial venture advancing Indian trade; and being naturally aggressive, he was not averse to pushing western interests to the point of war. While Virginia officials were willing to go to this extreme, they found the objects of the war aroused slight popular support.

Virginia's population in 1750 was located in three areas: the tidewater district, fairly thickly settled, given over to specialized farming and devoted to tobacco growing; the piedmont above the fall line of the rivers, more sparsely populated than the tidewater, absorbed in agricultural pursuits, not given over to one product, but producing chiefly grain, hogs, and cattle for the tobacco plantations and the West Indies; the frontier beyond the Blue Ridge, thinly inhabited, the people busily engaged in securing a meager existence by primitive agricultural methods.

Not until about 1700 were the best sections of the lowlands taken up for reserves in the great plantations, thereby creating a shortage of land.[1] In 1720 Spotsylvania and Brunswick counties in the piedmont were the frontier.[2] Soon special inducements, such as free grants of 1,000 acres to families under headrights and exemption from quitrents for seven years, were offered to secure settlers for the piedmont.[3] Goochland County was formed in 1728, and in 1729 proposals were made for establishing Richmond at the falls of the James river.[4] By 1730 scattered settlers had barely reached the Blue Ridge, and the Virginia Valley was untouched, as was much of the piedmont. The Carolina piedmont, a continuation of the Virginia area, was wholly unsettled. The Virginia Valley was geographically separated from the piedmont by the Blue Ridge, which served as a partial

[1] J. S. Bassett, *The Writings of Colonel William Byrd, in Virginia, Esquire*, p. xii.

[2] C. E. Kemper, "Early Westward Movement in Virginia," *Virginia Magazine of History and Biography*, XII, 337.

[3] F. J. Turner, *The Frontier in American History*, p. 91.

[4] *Ibid.*, p. 93.

barrier to settlement advancing through the piedmont
from the tidewater up the James, Rappahannock, and
York rivers.

While Virginia's migrating settlers were spreading
out into the piedmont, a stream of people was advancing down the valley from Pennsylvania after 1730. A
peninsula of settlement from Pennsylvania of a type of
people different in blood and customs from that of the
tidewater and piedmont was thrust down behind the Virginia settlements. The Germans, attracted by the cheap
land offered by Beverly, Borden, the Carters, Fairfax,
and others who had obtained it under the Virginia system of free grants by governor and council, moved south
from Pennsylvania.[5] After 1740 they were followed by
the Scotch-Irish.[6] The course of migration was from
north to south, on down across Virginia into the Carolinas, not from east to west. The moving peoples, barred
from the West by the mountains, followed the line of
least resistance.

During the decade before the French and Indian
War, Virginia's own migrating inhabitants had hardly
crossed the Blue Ridge. The colony still had sufficient
waste land to grant 1,000 acres at a time to individuals,
even though they came from outside of Virginia. Speculators, influential with the governor and council, obtained
grants of many thousands of acres. Though much of
the free land was taken up in this way, enough remained
to continue the system of free grants in the period after

---

[5] Turner, *The Frontier in American History*, pp. 101–2.

[6] *Ibid.*, pp. 104–5.

1740.[7] The Moravian missionaries, in their accounts of their travels through the Shenandoah Valley, reveal that a great part of the country was unsettled.[8]

Thus Virginia, during the period from 1740 to 1750, still had waste land for her people in the piedmont and in her valley, and the principal stream of immigration was not flowing toward the mountains, but down the valley toward the Carolinas. Need of more land or conflict of settlements west of the Alleghanies did not bring on the clash with the French.

Neither were the Virginians as a people interested in the Indian trade. The majority were farmers whose markets were in Europe. The greater part of their produce went to England, and their commercial outlook therefore was to the east rather than the west. The available data show how small a part of their economic life was identified with the Indian trade. Governor Dinwiddie in 1755 claimed an export trade of the value of £334,-000 sterling for the colony. Tobacco comprised £200,-000 of this amount. Wheat, corn, beef, pork, pitch, tar, iron, and wood totaled £115,000. Deerskins and furs, the articles received from the Indians, amounted to £20,-000.[9]

Probably Dinwiddie's estimate of the value of the fur trade, in which he was personally interested, was

[7] *Virginia Magazine of History and Biography*, XV, 117, 119–21, 237, 239; C. O. 5. 1423, "Virginia Council Journal," June 12, 1740, September 6, 1744, June 10, 1747, December 8, 1748.

[8] *Virginia Magazine of History and Biography*, XII, 56, 59, 141, 144, 145.

[9] *Dinwiddie Correspondence*, I, 386.

greatly exaggerated. The trade Virginia enjoyed was chiefly in skins, the least valuable part of the peltry trade. Before and during the opening of hostilities with the French an export of 10,000 deerskins in a year was a large amount.[10] In 1748 the average price per skin was slightly less than 4 shillings.[11] This would make the value of the overwhelmingly dominant article of Virginia's peltry trade about £2,000 in a single year. Even if Dinwiddie had been correct in his estimate, the fur trade constituted, according to his own figures, but one-tenth of the value of tobacco exported yearly. This export trade represented practically the entire fur trade of Virginia, for few of the skins were retained in the colony, which manufactured practically nothing. Moreover, the skins did not come from the West, where the conflict was taking place, but from the Southwest, and were brought into Virginia by the valley route. The Virginia traders were few in numbers and were practically the agents of the British merchants. The trade itself was not an industry belonging peculiarly to Virginia, but was a British interest. It benefited but a small number of the Virginians, and as a result Virginia as a whole was not vitally interested in it and was unwilling to support it.

Virginia was not concerned in a war fought for economic purposes which did not advance the economic needs of her own people, nor was she forced into the war

[10] "Journals of the Board of Trade," XXVI, 55, cited in P. S. Flippin, *The Royal Government in Virginia*, p. 349.

[11] Hanna, *Wilderness Trail*, II, 317; *Pa. Col. Recs.* V, 294, 328; *So. Ca. Gazette* (September 28, 1752).

for reasons of defense. The French were in the trans-Alleghany region, and the Virginia colonist knew it; but he had not experienced French and Indian raids, as had New York and New England. He could not but realize that as possible enemies the French and Indians were many days distant and were not likely to prove a real menace. In 1750, six years before war was declared, the average plantation owner of the tidewater could hardly consider the French a serious threat to the colony of Virginia. Nor did the frontier settler, separated from the Ohio by mountains and roadless forest regions, conceive of the French as an imminent menace to his home. The region was too remote, too many days' travel lay between the Shenandoah Valley and the Ohio. Mountains and forests helped effectively to divide the two frontiers. The Virginians, inexperienced in warfare with the French, evidently considered themselves safe from attack, as was shown by their inaction.[12] They had no particular interest involved, even if a few people of their colony were members of the Ohio Company whose prosperity depended on the successful thwarting of the French in the West.

Virginia, according to her conduct all through this period, was hostile to the Ohio Company and was unwilling to support a forward western policy at the probable cost of harrowing border warfare.[13] Washington considered that much of her opposition to the war was due to the belief that it was to advance the purposes of

[12] H. R. McIlwaine and J. P. Kennedy, editors, *Journals of the House of Burgesses of Virginia*, 1659–1776, 1752–55, *passim*.

[13] *Journals of Virginia House of Burgesses*, 1752–55, *passim*.

the Ohio Company.[14] Contrecoeur, commander of the French party which took the Ohio Company fort at the forks of the Ohio, was aware of this feeling when he said to the Virginians summoned before him: "Your Undertaking has been concerted by none else than by a Company who have more in View advantage of a Trade than to endeavour to keep the Union of Harmony which subsists between the Crowns of France and Great Britain."[15] Dislike of the Ohio Company made the Virginians suspicious of Dinwiddie. His membership in the company laid all his policy in the West open to the charge that it was motivated by personal and economic reasons for the benefit of the company rather than for the advantage of colony or empire.

Dinwiddie was appointed governor of Virginia just after the Crown, by its approval of the Ohio Company, was seemingly favorable to westward expansion. An ardent imperialist, he worked strenuously to forward British interests, and hoped to see the British Empire include ultimately the whole of North America. Like Shirley of Massachusetts, he considered the Great Lakes the strategic points for dominating the West.[16] He had imagination and earnestness, but was tactless, headstrong, impatient, and alive to the pecuniary advantages of his position. He completely alienated his assembly by stubbornly insisting on a fee for granting land patents at a time when he was asking his burgesses for votes of men

[14] W. C. Ford, editor, *The Writings of George Washington*, I, 414–15.

[15] *Pa. Col. Recs.*, VI, 29.

[16] *Dinwiddie Correspondence*, I, 496.

and money. His lack of administrative ability became evident after the opening of the war, when he attempted to organize the provincial military forces. Illness increased his incapacity, and before the termination of his governorship there was almost complete chaos in both the civil and military administration of Virginia. Dinwiddie was attempting to pursue a course which would doubtless benefit the colony at some future date, but nevertheless was at this time a dominantly British interest. He was aided by the council, made up of men prominent in the colony, appointed by the Crown, devoted to its interests.

While the governor and council were a force in the colony and supported the Crown's course, they could not place provincial resources at the service of the Empire. That power lay in the house of burgesses, the popularly elected branch of the government, representative of the people. The farming communities were represented in the house of burgesses by two members from each county, which in general was the unit of representation. The laws restricted suffrage to white male freeholders and householders, but they disqualified few of the white males because land was plentiful, cheap, and easily acquired.[17] The tidewater, the most thickly settled district, had the largest number of counties and elected a majority of the burgesses. As the tidewater voted, so most questions were determined. But the house can be considered in general to have represented Virginia's people. While there was inequality in representation be-

[17] E. J. Miller, "The Legislature of the Province of Virginia," *Columbia University Studies*, XXVIII, No. 2, 59–65.

cause the tidewater had a disproportionate share of burgesses, each county had two representatives and the idea
was strong in the colony that every burgess represented
all the people of Virginia.[18]

The votes of the house, by and large, can be said,
then, to have reflected the attitude of Virginia's voting
population. True, the house was composed largely of the
well-to-do and influential, but when the same men were
returned to office repeatedly they were evidently persons by whom the voters wished to be represented. The
class of people holding office could be expected to reject
or support the war accordingly as it reflected their economic interests and those of their constituents. As these
in the main did not coincide with the objects of the war,
their apathy is understandable. It could also be expected that the official body of the colony would be slightly
in advance of the people, particularly in the matter of
war. Its members were in closer touch with the situation, were better informed, felt a greater responsibility
for all the people of the colony, the alien frontier as well
as the English piedmont and tidewater. They would
probably be less affected by sectionalism and more sensitive to common needs of defense as war became dangerous to the outer fringe of the population but left the
vast body of people still untouched and apathetic. That
this was true was later evidenced when raids induced the
assembly to take measures for frontier defense which
were made futile by the indifference of the majority, as
yet unaffected by danger.

Through the early period of the war the assembly

[18] C. H. Ambler, *Sectionalism in Virginia*, p. 10.

clearly reflected the general unconcernedness of the population. To secure a complete understanding of the picture it is necessary to go back to 1752, when the assembly had its first opportunity to support the moves to occupy the West. In four sessions from 1752 to 1754 Dinwiddie repeatedly asked the house for measures to thwart the French.[19] He backed his pleas by statements of French plans and his measures to defeat them, by warnings of the consequences of French aggressions, by informing the burgesses of British aid of cannon and munitions, by citations of instructions from the Crown to have the assemblies grant supplies to block the French, and by appeals to their loyalty.[20]

The members of Dinwiddie's first assembly, 1752, were cognizant of his projects in the West and had unmistakable evidence of French intentions toward the Ohio through Céléron's expedition of 1749. Yet the house passed only one measure which could possibly be regarded as support of Dinwiddie's moves. In order to strengthen the provincial frontier by increased settlement, it voted to exempt settlers on the Mississippi waters from taxes for ten years.[21]

Another session called in the autumn of 1753 to secure supplies requisite to carry out the instructions of Lord Holdernesse showed the house reluctant to support Dinwiddie, although by this time the French had

---

[19] *Dinwiddie Correspondence*, I, 26; *Journals of Virginia House of Burgesses*, 1752-55, *passim*.

[20] *Journals of Virginia House of Burgesses*, 1752-55, pp. 104, 175-76, 190, 292.

[21] *Ibid.*, 1752-55.

advanced from Presque Isle southward into territory claimed by Virginia. The burgesses in no uncertain terms refused to increase his power over the militia.[22] They asked for information concerning the Indian treaties to which the colony had been a party, and for the instructions from Lord Holdernesse which the governor had cited to them at the beginning of the session.[23] Dinwiddie complied with the requests, though the one asking to see his instructions was extraordinary.[24] It was probably prompted by distrust of him, a natural consequence of his membership in the Ohio Company. The opposition aroused by this corporation can be read in the burgesses' suggestion that the governor grant land west of the mountains in small pieces free from the payment of rights and quitrents for 10 years.[25] Such a policy, had it been adopted, would have brought these free grants into competition with land of the Ohio Company and would have gone far to nullify the value of the company's western holdings. The only measure passed during this session favorable to the governor's western policy was similar to the act of 1752, with this difference: the time of tax exemption for settlers was increased to 15 years.[26]

Further aid was totally precluded by a dispute between executive and house. In 1753 Dinwiddie, with the consent both of the Board of Trade and his council, es-

[22] *Ibid.*, 1752–55, p. 115.

[23] *Ibid.*, 1752–55, pp. 1–6, 110.

[24] Flippin, *Royal Government in Virginia*, p. 85; *Dinwiddie Correspondence*, I, 139.

[25] *Journals of Virginia House of Burgesses*, 1752–55, pp. 115–16.

[26] Hening, *Statutes*, VI, 356.

tablished a 'fee of a pistole ($3.60) for taking out patents on land.[27] He imposed the fee in part to compel the registry of lands on the rent rolls and thereby make known land subject to quitrents; in part to increase his own income.[28] With the opening of the session of 1753 petitions of protest came in from five counties.[29] These were warmly supported by the burgesses, who opposed the fee system as a form of taxation beyond popular control and considered Dinwiddie guilty of using his position to line his pockets. On the other hand the burgesses were not without guile, for they attempted to shield constituents of theirs who, as estimated by Dinwiddie, held some 900,000 acres of land not yet brought to the rent rolls and so free of quitrents.[30] Dinwiddie refused to yield, defending the exaction of the fee as a royal prerogative and holding that waste land belonged to the Crown to be disposed of as it saw fit.[31]

Both sides were adamant and an unseemly dispute was permitted to prejudice the needs of defense until the burgesses finally sought to end the matter by sending Peyton Randolph, attorney-general, to lay their case before the central government. Without the consent of governor and council they voted him £2,500 Virginia curren-

[27] C. O. 5. 1367, letter from B. T. to Governor Dinwiddie, January 17, 1753.

[28] *Dinwiddie Correspondence*, I, 137; *Journals of Virginia House of Burgesses*, 1752–55, p. 154.

[29] *Journals of Virginia House of Burgesses*, 1752–55, p. 121.

[30] *Dinwiddie Correspondence*, I, 374; C. O. 5. 1328, letter of Governor Dinwiddie to B. T., December 29, 1753.

[31] *Journals of Virginia House of Burgesses*, 1752–55, p. 121.

cy as expense money.[32] Although the appropriation was
illegal, the burgesses were in a position to have their
wishes carried out, for John Robinson, the speaker of
the house, was also treasurer and agreed to make the
payment.[33] The house, to strengthen its position still
further and to guard against arbitrary action by the
governor, by resolve placed in Randolph's hands the
appointment of a permanent agent in England to look
after its interests.[34] With the question appealed to England, Dinwiddie could see no further purpose in continuing the session and prorogued the house.

The passion engendered by this quarrel gave strength
to the suspicion that Dinwiddie was influenced by a desire for personal gain rather than the welfare of the
frontier. Yet as the welfare of the frontier coincided
with the prosperity of the Ohio Company and the an-
tagonism of the burgesses was inimical to both, if Dinwiddie's wish was personal gain he was strangely inconsistent and lacking in foresight. He himself made the
statement that had he foreseen the reaction of the house
he would never have imposed the fee.[35]

When the third session of the assembly gathered in
the spring of 1754, the pistole fee question was in abey-
ance awaiting decision in London. Dinwiddie placed before the house Washington's report on the French plan
to occupy the Ohio.[36] Murders of Virginians in the up-

[32] *Ibid.*, 1752–55, pp. 168–69.

[33] *Dinwiddie Correspondence*, I, 160.

[34] *Journals of Virginia House of Burgesses*, 1752–55, p. 169.

[35] *Dinwiddie Correspondence*, I, 137.

[36] *Journals of Virginia House of Burgesses*, 1752–55, 175–76, 178.

per Potomac region, presumably by the French, had been reported.[37] Parts of the colonial militia were being mobilized and Trent's party had been sent forward to build the Ohio Company's fort at the forks of the Ohio.[38] Prompt action by the house was necessary if the Virginia claims to the trans-Alleghany region were to be upheld.

The burgesses gave half-hearted support to Dinwiddie. No greater control over the militia was granted, and the governor was compelled to rely upon voluntary enlistments.[39] A grant of £10,000 was woefully inadequate to secure and maintain an armed force, and even the expenditure of this amount was kept in the control of a committee of the house, thereby making the burgesses the real directors of the war.[40] In limiting the governor's military powers, the house simply followed an early precedent.[41] Though Dinwiddie objected to this infringement, he endured it to obtain the supply.[42] If the restriction stood alone or was associated with others in otherwise favorable legislation, its imposition would have meant nothing unusual. But it was accompanied by an inadequate money grant and absolute refusals to give the executive greater war powers. Later in the struggle, when war pressure was greater, the house, con-

[37] *Ibid.*, p. 176.

[38] *Ibid.*, 1752–55, pp. 175, 176.

[39] *Ibid.*, 1752–55, pp. 181, 182, 183; Hening, *Statutes*, VI, 421–22.

[40] Hening, *Statutes*, VI, 416–20; *Dinwiddie Correspondence*, I, 98, 101, 156.

[41] *Dinwiddie Correspondence*, I, 98.

[42] *Ibid.*, I, 98, 101.

fident of the ability and disinterestedness of the executive, removed this limitation on the powers of the governor. It may therefore be regarded as an indication of distrust and suspicion of the governor's western policy.

Despite this attitude toward himself and the manifest apathy to the western situation, a money grant had been made in this session which seemed to presage greater support, and Dinwiddie went forward courageously with his plans. Soon the inadequacy of funds forced him to call another session, which met in August. The task confronting Virginia was now intensified by French control of the Ohio secured through Washington's defeat. Instead of anticipating the French in the occupation of the territory, which would have been possible had action been taken in the spring, the British were now confronted with the necessity of driving them from their posts. Dinwiddie confidently expected that this situation would draw from the assembly generous support.[43] The burgesses cautiously began drafting a supply bill. They requested the governor to give them copies of all letters from England to himself and of all orders to the military officers.[44] Dinwiddie complied as far as he was able.[45] The house addressed Dinwiddie:

We cannot at all doubt but y't the other Colonies will exert themselves in a mutual assistance and unite with us in the comon Cause. But whatever they may do, we are determined on our Parts to withstand the impending Danger and to pursue every Measure in our Power to defeat those pernicious attempts of our Enemies,

[43] Ibid., I, 284.

[44] Journals of Virginia House of Burgesses, 1752-55, pp. 191, 192.

[45] Ibid., 1752-55, pp. 192, 193.

y't we may convince the World we have nothing more at Heart y'n a zealous discharge of our duty to the best of Kings and the sincerest regard for the Safety and true Int't of our Co't'y.[46]

A bill for £20,000 was passed and sent to the council.[47] Then Dinwiddie received a rebuff. The house committee on the expenditure of the £10,000 supply bill of the previous session refused payment for materials furnished by Dinwiddie for the independent companies sent by the Crown to aid Virginia in the Ohio campaign. The burgesses answered the governor's request for payment with a plea of poverty and courteously referred him to such supplies as were provided by Parliament for these forces.[48] Two days later the council rejected the £20,000 supply bill because it carried a rider forcing the council's assent to the £2,500 voted Peyton Randolph in 1753 for his expenses to England as advocate of the house against the pistole fee.[49]

The rider was an old device, employed in all the colonies to compel the prerogative bodies to accept an objectionable measure. The Virginia house, like the lower branches of the other colonial legislatures, took advantage of war needs to increase its powers. Neither council nor house would give way. The burgesses laid the blame for the defeat of the supply bill on the council, reproaching it for refusing to pay the expenses of the agent of the colony in England.[50] But Randolph was not the agent of the colonial government; he represented

[46] *Dinwiddie Correspondence*, I, 294.

[47] *Journals of Virginia House of Burgesses*, 1752–55, pp. 196, 201.

[48] *Ibid.*, 1752–55, pp. 201–2.

[49] *Ibid.*, 1752–55, p. 202.   [50] *Ibid.*, 1752–55, p. 203.

only the burgesses, and their statement of his purpose and position was hardly within the realm of truth.

Dinwiddie, finding his position impossible, now regretted his attempt to collect the fee,[51] for his insistence was defeating appropriations when most needed; but to retreat from his position would mean yielding on other matters until the burgesses usurped complete control. He attempted to find a way out of the dilemma by shifting responsibility on the home government and offered to assent to the rider provided it was placed in a separate bill with a proviso suspending its operation until the royal pleasure was known.[52] The burgesses refused his offer, feeling there was slight probability that the Crown would affirm the law.[53] The governor, convinced that they would do nothing unless unqualified assent was given their rider, called the declaration they had made at the opening of the session "only an unavailing Flourish of Words," and prorogued the house.[54]

Captain Peyronie, whom Dinwiddie had promoted at the request of the house, wrote Washington concerning this assembly, "I Shan't make Bold to Describe the proceedings of the house, which no doute you have had already Some hint of. I only will make use of these three expressions related to those of the oracle: furtim venerunt! invane Sederunt! perturbate Redierunt!."[55] And Washington knew no Latin!

[51] *Dinwiddie Correspondence*, I, 137.

[52] *Ibid.*, I, 324.   [53] *Ibid.*

[54] *Journals of Virginia House of Burgesses*, 1752–55, p. 205.

[55] S. M. Hamilton, *Letters to Washington and Accompanying Papers*, I, 39.

Both governor and house were responsible for the failure of the session. Dinwiddie, by his short-sighted imposition of the pistole fee, caused a quarrel which defeated what he most desired, support for the forward western policy. The burgesses subordinated imperial interests to the quarrel with the governor even in the face of defeat and hostile occupation of the Ohio district.

Apathy toward the West and distrust of Dinwiddie had marked every answer of the house to the governor's appeals for support in the first period of the war. Refusals of grants of money and of an adequate militia law, the request to grant land in small tracts, the call for papers on the governor's agreements with the Indians, the requests for his correspondence with the militia officers and for his instructions from the Crown, the pistole-fee quarrel, the inadequacy of the one supply, and the encroachment on the governor's prerogatives, give a clear picture of the lack of interest in royal policy and in the Ohio Company. Virginia's conduct affected the other colonies, for it furnished them an example.

When Dinwiddie received Washington's report on the French aim to occupy the Ohio Valley, he sent messages up and down the coast asking the other governors to aid Virginia against the French. But unfortunately for the success of his appeals the other colonies of the center and south were affected like Virginia by the shadow thrown across his requests by the Ohio Company and the evident purpose to forward its interests by force.

Pennsylvania, with her interest in the Indian trade and with lands west of the Alleghanies, might have been expected to aid in their defense, but refused in February, 1754, on the ground that the undoubted limits of the province had not been invaded. Like the other colonies, she had been instructed not to act beyond these limits, and the territory around the forks of the Ohio, then the scene of the struggle, was in dispute between herself and Virginia. Pennsylvania claimed that her action in this region would be equivalent to fixing the western limits of the province, which she did not feel qualified to do.[56] The members of the assembly asserted that the governor had not called upon them to resist hostile attempts, but had merely asked them to join forces with Virginia.[57] Repeated attempts by the governor during the year to secure aid for Virginia met with the same unfavorable response, although the possibility of raids on the frontier was recognized.[58] Hostility to the Ohio Company, indifference to general interest, Quaker principles, and more immediately a bitter quarrel with the executive over financial questions[59] influenced the assembly. The dispute of long standing involved essentially the question of political mastery in the province and continued in one aspect or another to block Pennsylvania's support of the war.

Maryland, with a definite western boundary and unable to benefit directly from the occupation of the Ohio

[56] *Pa. Col. Recs.*, V, 748.

[57] *Ibid.*

[58] *Ibid.*, VI, 25, 27, 40, 45, 134, 138, 140, 165, 166, 168, 186, 191, 193; *Votes and Proceedings of the House of Representatives of Pennsylvania*, IV, 308, 321.

[59] *Pennsylvania Votes of Assembly*, IV, 308, 321, 322, 324.

district, likewise declined to aid Virginia both in 1753
and 1754, basing her refusal on the ground that neither
Virginia nor any other colony was invaded nor subject
to any hostile attempt by the French.[60] In a third session of the assembly held in May, 1754, before Washington's defeat, the attitude of the delegates remained the
same, a quarrel between Governor Sharpe and his house
adding to the disinclination to vote supplies. The dispute arose out of the attempt of the house to appropriate for the supply the proprietor's income from hawkers'
and peddlers' and ordinary licenses.[61] The delegates
wished to have the money raised in Maryland used for
local affairs rather than for the enrichment of the Calverts, and the executive, the proprietor's representative,
governed by his instructions from the Calverts, was
equally determined to protect the proprietor's income
even at the expense of royal interests if necessary.[62] The
action of the Maryland delegates was similar to that of
the Virginia burgesses and Pennsylvania assemblymen.
They all placed constitutional questions above the general interest, insisted upon their own course, and used
the necessities of the situation to secure their political
ends.

But during the summer after Washington's capitulation, Maryland's frontier people, alarmed at the possibility of raids, threatened to move into the more settled
districts,[63] with a resultant decline in sales of proprie-

[60] N. D. Mereness, *Maryland as a Proprietary Province*, p. 318;
W. H. Browne, *Correspondence of Horatio Sharpe*, I, 38, 39.

[61] *Sharpe Correspondence*, I, 67-68.

[62] *Ibid.*, I, 174, 189, 190.   [63] *Ibid.*, I, 88-89.

tary lands on the frontier.[64] These factors secured a
compromise between governor and house. In a session
of the assembly held in July the delegates voted £6,000
to be used as Sharpe thought best.[65] They included
among the revenues for raising the appropriation one-
half of the fines from licenses for hawkers and peddlers.[66] Sharpe accepted the measure, but thinking he
had exceeded his powers, wrote the proprietor for instructions on the question of licenses.[67]

North Carolina responded to the call of Virginia
with a grant of £40,000 paper money, of which £22,000
was for war and £18,000 for other purposes. This latter
sum was not to be issued until royal consent was given.[68]
Of the former sum £10,000 was to support 750 men for
Washington's expedition, £5,000 for local defense, and
the remander for contingencies.[69] It is apparent that the
assembly took advantage of the military need to carry
through an expansion of paper money to meet provincial
requirements. It is also very likely that the assembly
felt that a grant for military service would cause the
Crown to view with favor the issue of the £18,000 additional paper money. This sum, with the £10,000 for war
purposes, would give the colony itself £28,000 of new
paper money. Indeed, it could reasonably be expected

[64] *Ibid.*, I, 161.

[65] *Ibid.*, I, 80, 81, 88, 89.

[66] *Ibid.*, I, 88–89.

[67] *Ibid.*, I, pp. 80, 131, 162.

[68] W. L. Saunders, editor, *The Colonial Records of North Carolina,*
V, 109.

[69] *Ibid.*

that the whole £40,000 would be expended locally, since North Carolina paper would be refused in the other colonies.

A second reason for the vote was the fact that the Ohio Company menaced neither North Carolina's western lands nor her Indian trade. The dividing line between her western lands and Virginia's had been surveyed and there was no conflict on that score. The Indian trade was not in the West, but in the South, with Creeks and Cherokees. North Carolina's interests were affected but slightly by the British advance in the West through the agency of the Ohio Company, and she needed a greater circulating medium. Her desire for soft money, rather than an imperialistic spirit, seems to have actuated her. In the absence of conflicting interests in the West, paper currency won support for Virginia.

Dinwiddie's forward policy in the West, his attempt to make treaties with the southwestern Indians, in fact any activities tending to disturb the settled conditions of the Indian trade, would be sure to meet with opposition from South Carolina. That colony enjoyed a large trade with the Creeks and Cherokees and even sent traders among the Ohio Indians. Like other colonies, she managed her own trade independently and to the exclusion of all others because the British government permitted such a course. The trade was valuable and South Carolina was acutely sensitive to activities tending in any way to influence it. She watched for and resented interference by the other colonies with the Indians on her frontier, whom she termed "her Indians." Dinwiddie was aware of this feeling and was most cautious in his letters to Governor Glen when he described the situation in the West and asked for aid. He was careful to explain the proposed conference at Winchester in 1754 with the southern Indians as merely a friendly meeting and not an attempt to form a new treaty, for he well knew that Glen would think a treaty meant trade relations.[70]

Despite Dinwiddie's diplomacy, Governor Glen probably read into the appeal a request for South Carolina to aid the Ohio Company, which he considered a possible rival of his colony in the Indian trade. Dinwiddie's alliances of 1752 and 1753 and proposed conferences with the Indians appeared to have no aims other than trade, because all Indian alliances were based on trade. Glen claimed that Virginia, prior to the formation of the Ohio Company, had no Indian alliances and therefore had no trade. In view of this situation, the recent alliances with the Indians were for trade and for the promotion of the Ohio Company.[71]

South Carolina was not in touch with the French; her trade was not menaced; and undisturbed Indian relations were to her advantage. The sanctioning of the Ohio Company by the Crown, the advance across the Alleghanies, the Indian treaties for land and trade made by Virginia's governor and council caused turmoil in the West, gave South Carolina a new rival, and created a situation unfavorable to her Indian trade.[72] Glen not

---

[70] *Dinwiddie Correspondence*, I, 61–63.

[71] *Ibid.*, I, 237, 272, 273, 274, 276.

[72] C. O. 5. 374, letter of Governor Glen to South Carolina Council, August 25, 1753; C. O. 5. 472, "South Carolina Commons House Journal," September 6, 1754.

only refused aid to Virginia, but even went farther when he blocked all southern Indian assistance from reaching her during the critical period in which the French were taking possession of the Ohio. When the Indians should have been in conference with Dinwiddie at Winchester, Glen persuaded them to remain away.[73]

The central and southern colonies, immediately in touch with the western frontier, with the exception of Virginia and North Carolina, had refused to support the Ohio Expedition. Virginia had given £10,000; North Carolina £10,000 paper money. In general the recalcitrant attitude of the several colonies was animated by opposition to British trade policy, by an absence of any obvious menace from the enemy, and by hostility to the Ohio Company. Dinwiddie's aims in the West savored too much of personal ambition. In the estimation of the other colonies, they advanced too greatly Virginia's power and ran counter to the interests of her neighbors. The British ministry, always willing to promote business interests but without any definite policy toward the Indian trade, had grasped at the opportunity offered by a private company to check the French and to further territorial and trade advantages. The Crown thus offered a course of conduct to the colonies which, when their jealousies, rivalries, and conflicting interests are considered, could scarcely hope to receive their support.

[73] *Dinwiddie Correspondence*, I, 273.

CHAPTER III

PRELIMINARIES OF BRITISH INTERVENTION

The indifference of the Virginia legislature to the war was paralleled by a like inertia in the military forces. The militia, based upon an act passed in 1738, was intended only for emergency protection against sudden invasion or insurrection and was to be dispersed when the crisis was past. This force was limited in its action to the local borders, and never was well trained. Military discipline, provided by the act of 1748, was in practice very loose. In fact the militia in Virginia, as in other colonies, was a historical tradition rather than a well-trained military body.

Realizing that his militia could not be used in an offensive move against the French, Dinwiddie attempted to create a little army by voluntary enlistments, but found it difficult. His proposal to grant lands west of the Alleghanies to men volunteering for service met with indifferent success. The frontiersman, an individualist, was only to be roused in defense of his own home. He found military life distasteful because it imposed on him a system of obedience and restraint at variance with his individualism. The inhabitants of the tidewater still regarded the conflict as far distant. As property owners they had their own interests demanding attention. In places there was such hostility to the war that the people even went so far as to prevent enlistment officers from obtaining recruits.[1] The troops secured were described as loose idle persons destitute of homes.[2] The act of 1748 which governed the discipline of the militia was also the only disciplinary measure controlling the army. It did not prescribe the death penalty, even for the grossest offenses. As a result desertion and insubordination were rife. Even the officers refused to obey commands, and left their posts as they pleased.[3] By the fall of 1754 Virginia's troops numbered but 140 men, North Carolina's, 50, and Maryland's, 50.[4]

The question of supplies for the troops constituted no less a problem than that of raising an army. Although Virginia was devoted to farming, she raised tobacco, not foodstuffs, in surplus.[5] Only her sparsely settled piedmont and frontier could furnish provisions for the troops, and these in limited quantities. It was difficult to convey the supplies collected in the interior to the army because the traffic lines in general were by the rivers to the sea, and, with the exception of the valley route, no good, well-established roads connected the various interior sections.[6] Indeed, even horses and wagons suitable for drayage purposes were lacking.[7] As a result of this situation the troops were often short of many necessaries. Dinwiddie, as head of the Virginia forces, created a commissary of stores and provisions which from a base at

---

[1] *Dinwiddie Correspondence,* I, 414.

[2] *Writings of Washington,* I, 42-43.

[3] *Dinwiddie Correspondence,* I, 147, 268.

[4] *Sharpe Correspondence,* I, 98-99.

[5] *Dinwiddie Correspondence,* I, 386.

[6] *Ibid.,* I, 489, 502-3; II, 49.   [7] *Ibid.,* I, 151, 489; II, 40.

Wills Creek was to furnish beef, flour, pork, and other supplies for five hundred men.[8] Preparations for provisioning the army were inadequate. The traders who promised supplies failed to keep their obligations. In short, by the fall of 1754 there was an almost complete breakdown of the commissary.[9]

Added to the deficiency of this branch of the service were money troubles. The balance of trade against Virginia caused a constant shortage of specie, and made her resort to tobacco currency, which circulated only within the colony and even there merely in the region about the warehouse where the tobacco was stored.[10] For this reason Virginia, in her purchases from the outside, was confined to specie, the supply of which was limited.[11] She obtained the money for her outside purchases and for general war purposes from taxes. These sources of revenue did not yield immediate returns, so the treasurer was forced to borrow and pledge the colonial revenues as security.[12]

The colony's borrowing was difficult from the first, and the funds obtained were exhausted by August, 1754.[13] The lack of money made it hard to secure enlistments, forced hardships upon the troops, who were without adequate clothing and blankets part of the time and

[8] *Ibid.*, I, 53.   [9] *Ibid.*, I, 220.

[10] W. Z. Ripley, *The Financial History of Virginia*, p. 153.

[11] *Sharpe Correspondence*, I, 177.

[12] *Dinwiddie Correspondence*, I, 109, 157, 163, 200, 219, 224, 268, 269.

[13] *Writings of Washington*, I, 131; *Dinwiddie Correspondence*, I, 278.

on occasions were even short of food.[14] Virginia's little
army by the fall of 1754 was demoralized and powerless.
Finally the service lost Washington, its only officer of
any ability, when Dinwiddie reorganized Virginia's
forces on the basis of an independent company and
made colonial officers inferior in standing to independent
company officers of like rank. Inefficient leadership,
ignorance of military affairs, shortage of ready money,
an insufficiently organized commissariat, dislike of military service, and lack of support from the colonial assemblies rendered the Virginia force useless. It was patent to all that success against the enemy could not be
expected from the colonies alone.

Dinwiddie realized this situation, and early in the
year requested money and troops from England.[15] In
May he appealed directly to the lords of the treasury
for funds to carry out his plans against the French.[16]
Indignant at the lack of foresight of the colonists, and
disgusted with their continual opposition, he advocated
action by Parliament to compel them to support the war.
This idea was expressed to Hamilton, governor of Pennsylvania; to the Earl of Albermarle, titular governor of
Virginia; Sir Thomas Robinson, secretary of state; the
Earl of Granville; and to Halifax, president of the
Board of Trade. The desire that Parliament force the
colonies to act became dominant with Dinwiddie and
found a permanent place in his correspondence.[17]

[14] *Dinwiddie Correspondence*, I, 220, 287–88.

[15] *Ibid.*, I, 95–96.

[16] *Ibid.*, I, 164.

[17] *Ibid.*, I, 203–4, 247–48, 250, 251, 256, 305.

To Robinson, secretary of state, Dinwiddie characterized the colonists as

. . . . extremely obstinate and self-opinionated, and at the
same Time infatuated to be so inactive and Indolent, w'n the
Enemy is so near our Frontiers, nay, I may say among our Settlers,
as they have robbed many of them of their Cattle and Corn, yet
they are not [to] be aroused to a proper Spirit for their own
Preservat'n and [are] at the same Time undutiful in not obeying
the com'ds of the best of Kings. On the whole I do think it inprac-
ticable to conduct any Expedition with a dependence of Supplies
from Assemblies in this Part of the World. They have all been
obstinate, refractory, and disobedient till lately, M'yl'd voted
£6,000 and N. Y. £5,000 their Monies, w'ch is only trifling with an
Affair of this Consequence, and I am strongly of Opinion y't with't
proper aid from G. B. of Men, Money and Ordnance Stores y't
the French in 8 Mo's will be so strong y't it will be difficult to root
them out from the Ohio and if allowed a quiet Settlem't there, I
fear their Views are to be Masters of All this Cont't.[18]

A regular stream of advice of this kind proceeded
from Dinwiddie to personages in England.[19] Sharpe and
other governors added their complaints to his. Sharpe
advocated that Parliament should raise funds for defense by poll taxes, duties on imports of arms and liq-
uors, excises and stamp taxes.[20] Other governors favored
action by Parliament and a consequent curtailment of
the powers of the assemblies. While these complaints
and recommendations were not acted upon at once, they
undoubtedly strengthened opinion that the colonies
would not tax themselves and perhaps had a part in de-

[18] *Ibid.,* I, 324–25.

[19] *Ibid.,* I, 203, 250–51, 284, 298–301, 322–27, 330, 333, 334, 335.

[20] *Sharpe Correspondence,* I, 99.

termining Great Britain to push her interests in America more aggressively.

Already in the fall of 1753 the colonial situation had induced the Crown to call the Albany Congress of June, 1754, to consider the questions of frontier defense, Indian alliances, and the regulation of the fur trade.[21] Although the primary aim of the British government was not a union, the colonists, when they assembled, discussed one, for union was essential to the desired end. In the Albany plan the essential feature was a central authority with control over all Indian affairs, power to raise and pay troops, build forts, and equip vessels.[22] The scheme was acceptable to neither Crown nor colonies.

Meanwhile the ministry, impressed by the growing seriousness of the situation in America, did not wait for the results of the Albany Congress. Although his action was not known in the colonies until much later, the secretary of state on June 14 directed the Board of Trade to present a scheme of union for the American colonies.[23] In August, 1754, the Board responded with a report which advocated placing military and Indian affairs under the control of one officer appointed by the Crown, and suggested the creation of a congress of one commissioner from each colony. This congress was to agree upon a military establishment and to apportion the quotas of men and money among the colonies for its support.

[21] *New York Colonial Documents*, VI, 799, 800–801.

[22] *Writings of Franklin*, III, 203–26.

[23] Root, *Pennsylvania and Great Britain*, p. 301; Beer, *British Colonial Policy*, p. 24.

While the Board was formulating this plan, the ministry took further action to improve conditions in the colonies. The pleas for aid were answered when in the early part of July assistance in arms and money was ordered for Dinwiddie. He was doubtless chosen as recipient because the ministry was not yet prepared to make an outright appropriation of money. It had to be repaid, and Virginia was in a better position to do so than the other colonies because of the royal revenue derived from the tax of two shillings on every hogshead of tobacco exported. This was ordinarily appropriated for government expenses, such as officials' salaries and contingent charges of government.[24] Also, as a royal colony, Virginia was more closely allied with the Crown and might prove more amenable in paying the debt. But Dinwiddie had shown his inability to secure the colonial assistance necessary for Great Britain's forward measures, and in the same month he was replaced by Horatio Sharpe, governor of Maryland, as head of the war forces of the central and southern colonies.[25] The objections raised against Dinwiddie could not be brought against Sharpe. His colony, unlike Virginia, had definite western boundaries and had no claims to western lands. In contrast to Dinwiddie, he was a man of military training and had no personal affiliations with the unpopular Ohio Company.

In October, 1754, Sharpe received the news of his appointment, and soon after he held a conference with

[24] *Dinwiddie Correspondence*, I, 353; Flippin, *Royal Government in Virginia*, pp. 230–31.

[25] *Sharpe Correspondence*, I, 73–74.

governors Dinwiddie of Virginia and Dobbs of North Carolina at Williamsburg, Virginia. The governors decided on a fall and winter campaign against the French, determining in case of success to build a fort opposite Fort Duquesne, and if their forces were increased to move against the French posts on the Great Lakes in the spring.[26] The plan had two objects: the safety of the frontier and the defeat of the French project to control the interior by a line of posts from Canada to New Orleans.[27] The ambition of the governors had gone beyond the forks of the Ohio and aimed at the real strategic points of western control, the Great Lakes.

In order to insure success for the scheme, aid was requested from Robinson, secretary of state.[28] This request was one of the series of repeated and insistent appeals which the governors had been transmitting to the Crown. When it was made, the aid granted early in July was on its way and was received by Dinwiddie in November, 1754. It consisted of 2,000 stands of arms, £10,000 specie, and an additional £10,000 credit. The loan furnished Dinwiddie with ready funds and placed the stamp of Crown approval on his work in the West.

The much-needed assistance was welcome, but men and additional money were required for the success of the governor's plans. They could only be obtained from the colonial legislatures. Dinwiddie summoned his assembly with better chances than ever before of securing support for vigorous measures in the West. Dinwiddie thought the aid from England would impress the bur-

[26] *Ibid.*, I, 104-6.

[27] *Ibid.*, I, 117.   [28] *Ibid.*, I, 104-6.

gesses favorably.[29] His requests evidently had royal approbation and would no longer be considered as a result of his membership in the Ohio Company. The disasters to Virginia's forces, the unsettled condition of the frontier, and the absence of a constitutional quarrel with the governor influenced the burgesses to assume a more favorable attitude toward a struggle not of their own creation or choice. The decision of the Board of Trade on the pistole fee had been received in the colony. While it was mainly in Dinwiddie's favor, certain concessions were made to the burgesses, who, either satisfied with the compromise or perhaps feeling that they had carried the controversy with the governor beyond the point of wisdom, accepted it as final.[30] Dinwiddie was soon on friendly terms with John Robinson, speaker of the house, and Peyton Randolph, the attorney-general, formerly his most prominent opponents, both members of the tidewater clique, the dominant body in the Virginia house.[31] Under these favorable circumstances the burgesses in the October-November session of the assembly, 1754, voted Dinwiddie £20,000. Like the prior supply of February, 1754, it was to be raised by borrowing.[32] The house, according to precedents, continued its voice in military affairs by placing a committee of burgesses in control of the expenditure of the appropriation.

In addition to money grants, if Virginia were to do her part in the war, troops had to be provided. Dinwiddie, ever since his arrival in Virginia, had desired a

---

[29] *Dinwiddie Correspondence*, I, 353.

[30] *Ibid.*, I, 363, 370, 373–74.

[31] *Ibid.*, I, 376, 409, 492–93.   [32] Hening, *Statutes*, VI, 435–37.

military establishment whose use would not be restricted
to the settled parts of the province. He favored the re-
placement of the general militia by a force of 2,000 men,
wholly under the governor's control; but knowing his
ideas were unlikely to be accepted, he merely asked for
the drafting of vagrants into service.[33] The assembly
complied with this request, and men for the army could
now be secured by voluntary enlistment and by draft of
vagrants.[34] In the light of past experience, if they were
to be useful, better discipline than was possible under
the law of 1748 had to be attained. The house appointed
a committee to bring in a bill for the prevention of mutiny and desertion.[35] The committee was appointed 10
days before the prorogation of the house, but no record
of its action appears on the journal. The burgesses' distrust of executive power, a part of their English heritage,
augmented by the conditions and interests of colonial
life, made them unwilling to submit Virginians to the
governor's coercive military authority.

A war waged by a democracy, if it is to be successful, requires a concentration of power in the hands of
the executive. This entails sacrifices by the citizens
which are only possible when they have the objects of
the conflict much at heart. Although better relations between the house and governor, together with English
aid, contributed to make the burgesses support Dinwiddie's efforts by granting a small amount of money, by
permitting citizens to volunteer, and by drafting va-

[33] *Dinwiddie Correspondence*, I, 367.

[34] *Journals of Virginia House of Burgesses*, 1752–55, p. 222.

[35] *Ibid.*, 1752–55, p. 217.

grants, they refused to give him the powers necessary to make the contributions effective. Virginia's interest in the extension of the empire was not great enough and the question of defense was not sufficiently vital to make her co-operate adequately with the Crown in aggressive western measures.

The governors of the other colonies also called their legislatures to secure aid for the campaign against the French. Imperial interests were now in the foreground, and neither the private claims of some one company nor even of a colony could be urged as a reason for refusing support. Pennsylvania made no grant in either her October or December session because of differences between governor and assembly.[36]

Maryland's legislature met in December and had before it the example of Virginia in November and of Pennsylvania in October. A new house had been elected, and there was a reasonable expectation that Maryland, with her governor in supreme command of operations, would be willing to vote supplies. But the governor had recently received an instruction from the proprietor forbidding him to assent to another bill appropriating money from licenses,[37] and the supply bill drawn up by the delegates included these forbidden revenues. It also added more paper money to the amount in circulation. These provisions made the measure objectionable to the council and defeated it.[38] In the Baltimore proprietary,

[36] *Pennsylvania Votes of Assembly*, IV, 328, 333, 335, 338, 342–43, 350–52, 382.

[37] Mereness, *Maryland as a Proprietary Province*, p. 323.

[38] *Sharpe Correspondence*, I, 158–59, 161–62.

as in Pennsylvania, constitutional differences prevented the possibility of favorable action.

North Carolina's assembly voted £8,000 of her un-issued paper for one company of one hundred men for Virginia and one of fifty men for the frontier's defense.[39] South Carolina, with Glen for governor, could not be expected to co-operate with the other colonies. Dinwiddie wrote of him, "He appears to be a wrong-headed Man, and the only Gov'r on this Cont't y't finds fault with my Conduct, and draws Conclusions from our late Misfortune near the Ohio."[40]

British imperial interests, though divorced from the objectionable features of private gain, had failed to rally adequate support in America. The colonies had shown themselves uninterested in the West, and the exigencies of defense were not yet great enough to make them act. Sharpe, during his ephemeral leadership, could do nothing because of colonial apathy. Such a situation awakened Great Britain to the fact that her active leadership in the New World was needed if her forward measures in the West were to be properly supported.

[39] *North Carolina Records*, V, 243–44, 312–13.
[40] *Dinwiddie Correspondence*, I, 375.

CHAPTER IV

BRADDOCK'S EXPEDITION

After receiving the Board of Trade's report in August, 1754, the ministry determined to accept its essential feature, a unified command of both the military and Indian affairs.[1] It definitely set its course on western expansion and decided to take a more active part in the American struggle. Instructions to the governors, issued in October, were received in the colonies near the opening of the new year. Two regiments of five hundred regulars each were to be sent to America. These forces, after their arrival, were to be recruited to the standard number of men.[2] The colonial governors were instructed to raise two additional regiments, to be commanded by Sir William Pepperell and Governor William Shirley, and to furnish food and necessaries for the army while it was in active service. All expenses of a purely local nature, arising within the separate colonies, were to be met by them individually, while those of a general character were to be paid from a common fund to be created by grants from the colonial assemblies and used particularly to raise troops. This arrangement which Secretary of State Robinson instructed the governors to secure was intended to last only until a more efficient

[1] Beer, *British Colonial Policy,* pp. 25–26; Alvord, *Mississippi Valley in British Politics,* I, 117–18.

[2] *Pennsylvania Archives, 1st ser.,* II, 203–7.

58

scheme of union could be determined upon by which the colonies might provide for their own defense.[3] General Braddock, a British officer of long service, was appointed commander-in-chief of the American forces and commissary of Indian affairs. The instructions to the governors caused the abandonment of the Williamsburg scheme of operations under which the colonies had been acting. The southern governors, however, continued their preparation for an attack on Fort Duquesne, for everything indicated that the new general's plan of campaign would have as its chief object the expulsion of the French from the Ohio. The success of the expedition depended largely on the interest taken in it by the colonies and the thoroughness of the preparations made by them.

The colonial governors were kept busy during the winter and spring of 1754 and 1755 in performing the duties required by their instructions. Dinwiddie could give the most effective aid because his assembly had given him a working fund of £20,000. The task of provisioning the expedition was turned over to him. He secured some of the needed materials from Virginia and North Carolina, but the bulk of supplies came from Pennsylvania.[4]

Although there were some complaints, the work of provisioning the army was fairly well done. But Dinwiddie had very little assistance in this task from the governments of the other colonies. In Pennsylvania he

[3] *Sharpe Correspondence*, I, 107–9.

[4] *Dinwiddie Correspondence*, I, 448, 454, 463, 478, 488, 503, 517, 523.

was aided greatly by Benjamin Franklin, who secured for the army much-needed horses and wagons.[5] Other individuals in that colony, as a matter of pure business, furnished large quantities of supplies at an exorbitant price without any co-operation from the colonial government.[6] Braddock's army was maintained, not by support given from sympathy with British aims in the West, but by the efforts of Dinwiddie, who had the money and could pay the necessary prices.

Another duty of the governors was to raise troops for the proposed campaign. Because of a relatively numerous population the demands on Virginia were heavy. The troops were secured by voluntary enlistment and by drafting vagrants. Voluntary enlistment in the absence of enthusiasm for Great Britain's policy continued to be an inadequate method of raising troops, either in the thickly settled regions or in the sparsely populated areas. Enlistments came in slowly; and the colony, to promote them, employed recruiting officers who went through the country offering bounties for recruits. The results were poor, for the officers, receiving a certain sum for each man enrolled, were interested largely in the money returns and enlisted many who could be of no possible service.[7] Then, too, the act drafting vagrants cast odium on the service, which undoubtedly added to the disinclination of the people to volunteer and retarded the raising of the forces. While the measure may have added to the number of men in the ranks, it restricted the enlistment

[5] *Pennsylvania Archives, 1st ser.*, II, 294–96, 310, 322.

[6] *Ibid.*, II, 335.

[7] *Dinwiddie Correspondence*, I, 470, 482, 483, 504–5.

of desirables and greatly lowered the usefulness of the army. The unpromising body of men secured in this manner comprised the Virginian army in the Braddock expedition.

The governors also had to defend the borders of their colonies while the expedition against Fort Duquesne was being mobilized, but no serious attacks were made on the Virginia frontier until Braddock's army met defeat.[8] The French were in possession of the Ohio district and conceded England's right to the eastern slope of the Alleghanies. They could well afford to remain on the defensive, leaving to England whatever opprobrium there was in that day for attacking the territory of a nation with which relations were supposedly peaceful. The threat of Braddock's army and a sense of their own weakness likewise deterred the French from taking the offensive. Despite their inactivity, rumors of their strength and intentions to attack the English frontier ran through the colonies from time to time and occasioned alarm.[9]

Virginia's frontier was long, considerably exposed, and in time of hostility needed a large number of men in constant readiness to repel invasion. Border defense during Braddock's expedition rested primarily on the militia, but that force, besides being woefully inefficient, could not be kept constantly under arms. The colony decided to supplement it by a ranger system. The assembly in June, 1755, granted £2,000, out of an appro-

[8] *Pennsylvania Archives, 1st ser.*, II, 362–63; *Journals of Virginia House of Burgesses, 1752–55*, p. 286.

[9] *Dinwiddie Correspondence*, I, 485; II, 51, 67, 70.

∫

priation of £10,000 paper money, to raise and maintain three companies of rangers of fifty men each for service in the frontier counties. The rangers were exclusively for border protection, and were not to be sent out of the colony nor to be subject to martial law. They were to be raised, if possible, by voluntary enlistment but if that method were not successful, by draft from the three western frontier counties of Augusta, Frederick, and Hampshire.[10]

The colony as a whole, including the three before-mentioned counties, contributed the £2,000, but the most heavily populated area, the tidewater, a region interested in agriculture with the dominant voice in the assembly, not only refused to draft its own people for war purposes, but would not even acknowledge frontier defense as a part of the obligation of its man power to the people as a whole. This selfish course may have been actuated in part by the feeling that the frontier was composed of Germans and Scotch-Irish, people of different blood and religion from that of the tidewater. It should certainly be considered as evidence of lack of sympathy with British interests in the West, an opinion that the war was of small moment, and the belief that, with Braddock's troops advancing, the question of defense against French and Indians could easily be cared for by the sparsely populated counties immediately concerned. Dinwiddie also must have felt a sense of security in the British advance, for, absorbed in his tasks connected with the British army, he delayed raising the rangers until Braddock's defeat let loose a swarm of French and

[10] Hening, *Statutes*, VI, 465–66.

Indians in retaliatory raids on Virginia's helpless border.[11]

The contemplated attempt of the British on Fort Duquesne, like all expeditions in America, needed Indians for scouting and brush fighting. Until Braddock arrived in the colonies, the governors continued in charge of Indian relations. Although the Ohio and Pennsylvania Indians had been friendly to the English, after Washington's defeat in 1754 they quite generally deserted to the successful French. This situation made it necessary to look to the Iroquois and southern Indians for alliances. General Braddock, after his arrival, sent William Johnson to the Iroquois to win their active aid, but he had little success.[12] Dinwiddie was expected to secure assistance from the southern Indians. His instructions required him to work with Governor Glen in giving presents to the Cherokees and in building a fort in their country to secure their aid. He and Glen were to agree on the amount to be expended on the fort, the sum determined on to be drawn from the funds loaned by England.[13] As repayment of this loan fell solely on Virginia, the fort would cost South Carolina nothing, and located among the Cherokee Indians would benefit her more than any other colony.

This was Glen's opportunity, and his particularism completely dominated his demands on Dinwiddie. He estimated that three hundred men were necessary to build the fort, and claimed the right to draw on the

[11] *Journals of Virginia House of Burgesses*, 1752–55, p. 291.

[12] *Dinwiddie Correspondence*, II, 9–10.

[13] *Ibid.*, I, 484.

£10,000 credit for £7,000 without even an understanding with Dinwiddie. In his aim to advance South Carolina's interests Glen had greatly overestimated both the force and the amount of money necessary to build the Cherokee fort. Dinwiddie thought it could be built for one-third Glen's estimate.[14] Although he was willing to pay the expense as directed, he could not but feel that it should be borne by South Carolina. The disagreement between Glen and Dinwiddie over this question, increased by their distrust of each other because of the controversy in the preceding year over the southern Indians, developed into an acrimonious quarrel which prevented any co-operation between them.[15] Virginia's governor, convinced that he could not work with Glen, sent messengers directly to the southern Indians.[16] Glen again took measures to forestall him and prevent the Indians from assisting Braddock. When they should have been on their way to join Dinwiddie, they were at Charleston in a conference with Glen.[17]

Dinwiddie's task of preparing for the Braddock ex-

[14] *Ibid.*, I, 484–85.

[15] Dinwiddie to James Abercrombie, the London agent, Williamsburg, January 18, 1755: "He is altogether the strangest possitive assum'g Man I ever corresponded with, and there I leave him" (*Dinwiddie Correspondence*, I, 508); Dinwiddie to Governor Dobbs, May 5, 1755: "I think it not very modest in him to desire such a Sum but surely he is wrong in his Head" (*ibid.*, II, 24); Dinwiddie to William Wragg of South Carolina: "Mr. Glen's Method of Writ'g is happily peculiar to himself, his Criticisms inconsist't with Truth and really of an unusual dictatorial Style y't I cannot answer his Let's [but] with Reluctance" (*ibid.*, II, 28).

[16] *Ibid.*, II, 76.

[17] *Ibid.*, I, 509; II, 55, 188.

pedition was made more difficult by Virginia's continued lack of hard money. The expedition necessitated the purchase of supplies from the other colonies. The unusual volume of purchases from her neighbors,[18] the borrowings of the treasurer—for Virginia was raising the £20,000 voted in 1754 by these methods—[19] and the natural tendencies of the people to hoard in war time soon exhausted the colony's scant supply of specie.[20] The money and credit Dinwiddie received from England and the sale of bills of exchange in Philadelphia[21] relieved the situation for a time, but it was soon as bad as ever.

The disappearance of specie did not cause the Virginia people as a whole very great hardship because the domestic needs for money, which were very slight due to the agricultural nature of the colony and the absence of towns, were easily satisfied by the tobacco currency. But the task of securing specie, made increasingly difficult by the growing war operations, became practically impossible, and the colony was unable to meet its war obligations. Reimbursement could no longer be made for supplies, and the pay of the troops fell months into arrears.[22] It was evident that war needs required a greater circulating medium, and paper money seemed to be the only means at hand. This recourse had been con-

[18] *Ibid.*, I, 458, 478, 503, 517.

[19] *Ibid.*, I, 520; II, 85.

[20] *Ibid.*, I, 477, 503.

[21] *Ibid.*, I, 478, 503, 510, 517.

[22] *Sharpe Correspondence*, I, 201; *Dinwiddie Correspondence*, I, 519, 520; II, 81.

sistently avoided by the Virginians,[23] but it was being forced upon them by a war which they had not favored. Probably their unwillingness to embark on a policy of issuing paper money had something to do with the burgesses' disinclination to make large grants of money in the session held for the express purpose of aiding Braddock. As a result of the financial stringency Dinwiddie found himself handicapped not only by a greatly contracted circulating medium but by the assembly's hesitation to make any adequate grants of money for war purposes.

A further handicap affecting the colonies was the trade carried on by some of them with the French. In a letter to Robinson, January, 1755, Dinwiddie explicitly charged New York and Pennsylvania with furnishing supplies to the French, thus enabling them to hold the Ohio district. Louisburg, he maintained, was the center where English food products were exchanged for French rum, molasses, and sugar. Thence the English goods went to Quebec. He advocated that flour, bread, pork, and "Pease" be listed among the enumerated products, which would have prevented their shipment to foreign countries.[24] Morris, of Pennsylvania, corroborated Dinwiddie's charges, though he attempted to clear his own colony, the largest provision-producing province, of the trade.[25]

Further confirmation of this commerce is found in

[23] Ripley, *Financial History of Virginia*, p. 153.
[24] *Dinwiddie Correspondence*, I, 473.
[25] *Pa. Col. Recs.*, VI, 336–37, 338.

a letter from Morris to Braddock concerning a fort planned near Crown Point:

But I do not think that the Governments of New York, New Jersey, or Pennsylvania can be prevailed upon to do their's. The Assemblys of the two last are under the Influences of Quaker Councils, from whom nothing good is to be expected; and as to New York, the Albany Members, who have a very great Influence in their Legislature, are concerned in a very pernicious but profitable Trade that is carried on between Albany and Crown Point, and it is to be feared that they would rather see the former in the Hands of the French than contribute to annoying the latter. By that Trade the French are furnished with the most material Articles of their Indian Trade, and are thereby enabled fully to supply them, which they could not otherwise do. And within these few Months great Quantities of Gunpowder have been brought up in this Town and New York, and I am told sent from Albany to Crown Point, there being only twelve Miles Land Carriage between them. . . . .[26]

Although Virginia produced but few articles in any quantity needed by the French, Dinwiddie laid an embargo on provisions as a precedent for the other governors.[27] Massachusetts passed an act which for three months required masters to give bonds to carry provisions to British ports only.[28] The trade with the enemy, although unpatriotic, was not illegal, for the two countries were not officially at war. Therefore it was futile for one colony to take measures not concurred in by the others, for the French could still obtain supplies from the colonies refusing to prohibit the trade. Pennsylva-

[26] Morris to General Braddock, Philadelphia, March 12, 1755, *Pa. Col. Recs.*, VI, 338.

[27] *Dinwiddie Correspondence*, I, 526-27.

[28] *Pa. Col. Recs.*, VI, 309; *Sharpe Correspondence*, I, 169.

nia's governor in March, 1755, required a bond of all masters obliging them to discharge cargoes of provisions in British ports or in countries in amity with England. The assembly sanctioned the executive act by a law of three months' duration, and later continued it for a year. As the act did not preclude the indirect trade and nothing more could be obtained from the legislature, the governor laid a general embargo until further notice.[29]

Although some of the colonies prohibited direct exportation to French ports, the enemy secured provisions from the English colonies indirectly through neutral ports in the Spanish and Dutch West Indies. This trade was not stopped before the opening of formal war. The colonies, jealous of each other, were only willing to pass acts dependent on similar legislation by the others. New York, Pennsylvania, and New Jersey in turn enacted laws to prevent the indirect trade, but each with the proviso that its act should not become operative until the neighboring colonies had passed similar measures. As Delaware would only pass a law for a general embargo for but one month, the legislation of the other colonies was prevented from going into effect.[30] The commercial classes of each colony were too particularistic to stop such a profitable business, even for the safety of their own colony's frontier and the welfare of the empire.

These classes continued the trade even after the declaration of war. The governors had formal instructions to prevent it, but could not accomplish much, as their orders in this case ran counter to the economic in-

[29] Root, *Pennsylvania and Great Britain*, p. 78.
[30] *Ibid.*, pp. 79–83.

terests of the colonies. Even the Parliamentary act of 1757, prohibiting during the war the exportation of provisions from the colonies "unless to Great Britain or Ireland or to some of the said Plantations and Colonies,"[31] backed by the British fleet, was not able wholly to prevent this treasonable commerce.

One of the most important duties of the governors was to secure appropriations from their assemblies to maintain colonial troops and the common supply ordered by their instructions. Certain funds were already available, for Virginia and North Carolina had granted aid in the fall and early winter which, intended for the Williamsburg plan, had been diverted to that of Great Britain. In order to secure additional supplies necessary for a successful pursuance of the Crown's project, the governors placed the instructions from the secretary of state before their assemblies.

Pennsylvania's legislature which had convened December, 1755, received them in January. Unfortunately it was quarreling with the governor over the right to view his instructions, and voted only £5,000. The appropriation, made by resolution and without the governor's consent, was to be used for the purchase of wagons and flour for Braddock's army.[32] Governor Morris in the March assembly appealed first to the loyalty of the legislators by announcing General Braddock's arrival and then to their interest in the colony's western development by informing them of roads to be built in the West, but all to no avail. The assembly voted

[31] *Pennsylvania Archives, 1st ser.*, III, 97.

[32] *Ibid.*, II, 250, 252–53.

a long-time issue of paper, which the governor would not accept.[33] After Morris refused the bill, the house voted £15,000 by resolution, £5,000 of it to repay the January grant for Braddock's army and the rest for the Massachusetts Bay troops.[34]

Maryland was even less willing than Pennsylvania to support the Braddock expedition. In February the delegates showed that they intended to follow Pennsylvania's example if that province refused to grant supplies. Governor Sharpe thought that there was a direct connection between the legislatures of the two provinces, and that the northern proprietary was responsible for much of his colony's recalcitrant action.[35] The house voted £10,000 paper money, and as usual "ordinary licenses" were included among the other revenues for sinking the paper. The council accordingly rejected the bill, which made the house declare, "The appropriation of ordinary license fine . . . . we are so firmly of opinion, is the undoubted right of the country, that nothing will ever induce us to give it up or do anything that may weaken that right."[36] The house definitely refused to vote money in any other way than as proposed in the bill, and after a month's session was prorogued.[37]

General Braddock arrived in Virginia in February, 1755, and called governors Shirley, Dinwiddie, Sharpe, Morris, and De Lancey into conference at Alexandria in

[33] *Pennsylvania Votes of Assembly*, IV, 382–83, 388, 390.

[34] *Ibid.*, IV, 391–92, 400.

[35] *Sharpe Correspondence*, I, 165.

[36] Mereness, *Maryland as a Proprietary Province*, pp. 323–24.

[37] *Sharpe Correspondence*, I, 189.

April. The council mapped out the whole campaign against the French in North America. Attacks were determined against Fort Duquesne, Niagara, and Crown Point. Braddock was to lead the expedition against Fort Duquesne, Colonel Willliam Johnson that against Crown Point, and Governor Shirley that against Niagara. The governors assumed the obligation of persuading their assemblies to establish a common fund for the payment of general expenses, and decided that Fort Duquesne after its capture should be garrisoned by colonial troops. In addition the conference voted that Pennsylvania, Maryland, and Virginia should pay for the erection of a fort on Lake Erie if such a post was later considered necessary.[38]

The results of the conference greatly encouraged Dinwiddie and aroused in him the most sanguine hopes of success. With the aid of British regulars he foresaw the capture of Fort Duquesne, a march to Lakes Erie and Ontario, and, joined by the New England regiments, the capture of Crown Point. This triumphant progress was in his opinion merely a reclaiming of the lands ceded to the English by the Treaty of Utrecht.[39] The Braddock expedition, he hoped, would be aided by the southern Indians, whom he imagined would immediately join the English when they heard of the arrival of British regiments.[40] Dinwiddie was a true believer in British invincibility and thought that British assistance would surely dispel all the difficulties of the colonies. He wrote

[38] *Ibid.*, I, 203–4.
[39] *Dinwiddie Correspondence*, I, 496.
[40] *Ibid.*, I, 509, 524.

Lord Halifax that he had advised Braddock to send the New England regiments against Niagara, to have New York reinforce Oswego, which was open to attack, and to seize the lake country after the capture of Fort Duquesne.[41] Dinwiddie, though somewhat optimistic, saw clearly the importance of the Great Lakes region to the colonies, not only for the frontier's defense, but for the control of the fur trade and the whole interior of the continent. But he was basing his hopes on his faith in the invincibility of British arms, not on his belief in the bounty of the Virginia assembly.

The first meetings of the assemblies in the other colonies in 1755 made Dinwiddie uneasy as to their effects on the Virginia burgesses.[42] He attributed much of the colony's disinclination to support the service to an opinion prevalent among the Virginians that they were dupes; they aided the expedition while the others, in equal danger, merely looked on.[43] Although the support given by Virginia was slight, she had done more than any other colony. When Braddock's forces were on the march, Virginia officials provisioned them, and Virginia troops were the only ones to accompany them in any considerable numbers. Virginia's frontier was left defenseless except for the militia, and even in this situation, had Pennsylvania and Maryland made adequate preparations for their own defense, Virginia would have received some protection from them because of her geographical location to the south. While Virginia had tried constantly to secure the co-operation of the southern

[41] Ibid., I, 527.

[42] Ibid., I, 525, 526, 527–28; II, 5, 16, 17, 46.   [43] Ibid., I, 525, 527.

Indians, her attempts had been frustrated by Glen's activities in defense of South Carolina's peculiar interest in the Indian trade.

Combined with these factors were two others which might well arouse animus in the minds of Virginians: Virginia's financial stringency increased by her need of purchasing provisions outside her own borders for the army; the trade with the French by Pennsylvania, Rhode Island, New York, and Massachusetts. Despite Morris' effort to clear his province, it was considered one of the worst offenders in both the direct and indirect commerce.[44] Although Pennsylvania should have been closely associated with Virginia in the war, she had practically refused all support. Certain of her citizens and those of other colonies were making profits in this pernicious trade and indirectly aiding the enemy Virginians were spending money, though in insufficient amounts, to subdue.[45] This situation, evident to the Virginians, must have discouraged the burgesses and adversely affected their grants of supplies.

In addition those Virginians interested in western trade and land, persons who were giving the war real support, were suspicious of the activities of Maryland and Pennsylvania in the West and saw in all their movements there an attempt to gain advantages at Virginia's expense. The war meant to the small imperialistic party

[44] Beer, *British Colonial Policy*, pp. 90–91.

[45] Both Dinwiddie and Morris thought colonial trade with the French furnished them with provisions, essential if they were to hold the Ohio. *Dinwiddie Correspondence*, I, 473; *Pa. Col. Recs.*, VI, 336–37, 338.

of Virginia the opening of the West through Virginia territory and the strengthening of the colony's hold on the advantages of Indian trade and territory. When one division of Braddock's army was sent through Maryland, Washington wrote Fairfax, "Those who promoted it had rather that the communication should be opened that way, than through Virginia; but I can believe that the eyes of the General are now open, and the imposition detected; consequently the like will not happen again."[46]

The opinion that the other colonies wanted communication to the West was well founded, for Pennsylvanians also were scheming to extend roads there. In the spring of 1755 individuals endeavored to make Braddock see that Pennsylvania would furnish a better base for operations against Fort Duquesne than any other colony. Richard Peters, secretary of Pennsylvania, wrote William Shirley, Braddock's secretary:

By Mr. Evan's Map, which he has enclosed in this Packet to you, the Country to the West of the Ohio will, I think be pretty well known, at least, well enough for your present Use. It will immediately occur to you that Shippensburgh, not Will's Creek, would have been the most convenient Place for the Camp, as well on acco[t] of health as Provisions, as nearness of Situation and Roads over the mountains, plentiful Supplies are to be had there, and you would have been as near your Place of destination, and have saved the Expense of Carriage, which is almost as much as the Price of Provisions.[47]

These maneuvers were known to Virginians and increased their feeling that Virginia was not being fairly

[46] *Writings of Washington*, I, 151-52.

[47] Richard Peters, secretary of Pennsylvania, to William Shirley, Braddock's secretary, May 12, 1755 (*Pennsylvania Archives, 1st ser.,* II, 309).

treated. Washington, in close touch with the situation and always very responsive to opportunities in the West, again wrote:

There is a line of communication to be opened from Pennsylvania to the French Fort Duquesne, along which we are to receive, after a little time, all our convoys of provisions, etc., etc., and to give all manner of encouragement to a people, who ought rather to be chastized for the insensibility to danger and disregard of their sovereign's expectation. They, it seems, are to be the favored people, because they have furnished what their absolute interest alone induced them to do, i. e., 150 wagons and an equivalent number of horses.[48]

As the campaign progressed Virginians became convinced that their northern neighbors, while not supporting the expedition, were attempting to profit to the utmost from it.

When Dinwiddie met his burgesses in May he laid the plans of the Alexandria conference before them, asked them to reimburse him for supplies furnished the regular troops at the command of the secretary of state, stressed the need of strengthening the colony's troops, and exhorted the burgesses to give their most serious attention to his requests.[49] The assembly passed two small grants totaling £16,000, of which £2,000 were allocated to maintain one hundred and fifty rangers for border protection.[50] Six thousand pounds were to be raised by a lottery, £10,000 by an issue of paper. With this issue the colony at last succumbed to the necessity

[48] Writings of Washington, I, 162.

[49] Journals of Virginia House of Burgesses, 1752–55, p. 232.

[50] Ibid., 1752–55, p. 288; Hening, Statutes, VI, 453–61, 461–68; see above, pp. 61–62.

of using paper money.[51] Braddock's common fund scheme, which would have made it impossible for the house either to control or require an accounting of the appropriation, evidently did not meet with the approval of the burgesses, for the expenditure of both grants was placed under the control of a committee of the house.[52] The measures were passed at different times during the session; the larger grant was made first, the smaller not until July 3, six days before the end of the session and too late to be of any value in the campaign.[53]

Dinwiddie met with less success in his other requests. The house failed to pass a measure for better discipline in the army, and denied Braddock's demand that the militia occupy Fort Cumberland and convoy supplies to the forces if necessary.[54] The burgesses gave the excuse that Cumberland was not in Virginia, and the militia could not legally be sent there. They held that convoys would require further funds, which the colony could not afford. They even expressed a hope that the governor would not add to their financial burdens by calling out the militia at this time, for any added expense would bring utter ruin upon the colony and preclude future grants of aid.[55]

Throughout the session Dinwiddie urged the house to support Braddock's expedition vigorously, but had no success aside from the two small money grants. At the

[51] Hening, *Statutes*, VI, 454, 467.
[52] *Ibid.*, VI, 460, 467.
[53] *Journals of Virginia House of Burgesses*, 1752–55, p. 288.
[54] *Dinwiddie Correspondence*, II, 41, 44.
[55] *Journals of Virginia House of Burgesses*, 1752–55, p. 267.

very close of the session, when Braddock's army had advanced beyond the frontier, a report that families on the border had been attacked[56] caused the governor to ask the house for more adequate frontier defense. The burgesses merely advised the use of the rangers provided for this purpose.[57] Convinced that it was impossible to secure further aid, Dinwiddie prorogued the assembly the second week in July.

When the work of that body is summed up it is evident that British aid, in the absence of an intense urge, failed to make Virginia enthusiastically support the Crown's forward policy. Money was granted only in small amounts, and the total sum was not complete until the close of the session. The scheme of a common fund was opposed because it ran counter to constitutional privileges gained through long struggle. Lack of experience and fear of military power again defeated the bill for increasing the efficiency of the army. Tradition circumscribed the use of the militia and left the frontier open to attack.

Besides Virginia, South Carolina was the only colony to vote supplies for Braddock after the Governor's conference at Alexandria. Even with Glen for governor, she made a nominal grant of £6,000.[58] The legislatures of Pennsylvania and Maryland met in June, while Virginia's assembly was in session, and thus were aware of the apathy of that body toward the western attack. In both proprietary provinces money grants for the Braddock expedition were defeated by the development of

---

[56] *Ibid.*, 1752–55, p. 286.   [57] *Ibid.*, 1752–55, p. 291.

[58] *Dinwiddie Correspondence*, II, 62, 77.

contests between governor and house in which neither would give way.[59] Pennsylvania's only measure against the French was the law sanctioning for three months the executive act preventing direct trade with the enemy.[60]

This survey shows that the assemblies of the five colonies concerned held a total of twelve sessions in preparation for Braddock's offensive and voted five grants of aid. Virginia, in two sessions, gave £36,000; Pennsylvania, in four sessions, but £5,000 for flour and wagons; North Carolina, in one session, £8,000; South Carolina, in two sessions, £6,000, and Maryland, in three sessions, nothing. The internal situation in the colonies was not extraordinary. Time-honored questions of dispute between governors and assemblies still held their places. So slight was colonial interest in the western attack that the representatives could not forbear to use their power over the purse to attempt encroachment on the powers of the governors.

The action of the provincial legislatures made evident that the colonies had no vital interest in the attempt to possess the Ohio and would not support it. The governors, disappointed over their apathy, recommended the same sort of measures to the Crown as they had in 1754. They agreed that parliamentary taxation was the only means left to raise money in the colonies for defense.[61] Dinwiddie had repeatedly censured the pro-

[59] *Pennsylvania Votes of Assembly*, IV, 409, 410, 414; *Sharpe Correspondence*, I, 190, 194–95, 218, 232, 233, 240.

[60] See above, p. 68; *Pennsylvania Votes of Assembly*, IV, 406.

[61] *Sharpe Correspondence*, I, 195; *Dinwiddie Correspondence*, I, 493.

prietary provinces for their recalcitrant acts.[62] The refusal by Pennsylvania and Maryland in January and February, 1755, had induced him to advocate changes in the proprietary constitutions, particularly in that of Pennsylvania.[63] When the Quaker colony in March, 1755, ridiculed the Crown's requests by making a grant for the Massachusetts troops and none for the Braddock expedition, he wrote:

I am sorry there are any Proprietary Gov'ts on y's Cont't, for they are litigiously wanton with their Liberties and Charters. I wish the Proprietors well, but I wish the Crown w'd make a proper Purchase from them, or at least take the Rules of Gov't into their own Hands, for I think there was never such monstrous ill-conduct from any set of People in Time of so great Danger. An Union of the Colonies is greatly to be desired, but even then these Colonies will continue obstinate and fractious, unless a general Tax is laid on all the Colonies by a British Act of Parliament.[64]

The letters of the governors reveal that in all the central and southern colonies the executives did not have the support of their legislatures, and that imperial interests were second to colonial aims. The plans they submitted to the Crown to force colonial support for Great Britain's forward measures, had they been adopted, would undoubtedly have met with resistance from provinces having the right of voting their own taxes in representative bodies. With war needs pressing it would have been dangerous to risk antagonizing the colonies, and the recommendations could not be followed out; but they had an effect in determining the British attempt at

[62] *Dinwiddie Correspondence*, I, 492, 507, 526; II, 16, 17, 46.

[63] *Ibid.*, I, 523-24.

[64] Dinwiddie to Halifax, Williamsburg, April 30, 1755, *ibid.*, II, 17.

the close of the war to find surer ways of raising money from the colonies.

In the midst of the governors' preparations for Braddock's army and while the colonial assemblies were debating to what extent they would support the Crown, the British regiments landed at Alexandria. After waiting a time there for recruits, they marched toward Wills Creek, one regiment through Maryland, the other through Virginia. The last of May, Braddock's army, accompanied by 450 Virginians, began the march over the Alleghanies. The colonists had little information about the French, but that little led them to expect an easy victory. The failure of British arms was a complete surprise and caused great consternation. The disaster in the south had a parallel in the north. According to the general plan, expeditions were pushed forward against Crown Point and Niagara. William Johnson attempted to take Crown Point and failed. Governor Shirley, in his campaign against Niagara, was likewise unsuccessful, partly because Braddock's defeat prevented expected co-operation and partly because the army could not secure supplies.

While the defeat of Braddock was in great part due to his own rashness and unwillingness to follow colonial methods of fighting, a share of blame must be borne by the colonies. Their assemblies had refused to vote the men and money which would enable the governors to co-operate in war measures. The two Carolinas did not have the wealth or population to support the war very strongly, but even in proportion to their strength their assistance was negligible. The real refusal to aid Braddock was in Virginia and the two proprietary colonies. Pennsylvania and Maryland turned a deaf ear to imperial policy in their opposition to proprietary claims. Their example reacted unfavorably on Virginia, lukewarm herself to the Crown's moves against the French. Alone of the southern colonies to give anything like consistent support to the war, Virginia voted insufficient aid and persisted in a denial to her Governor of sufficient military measures. In turn Virginia's indifferent support furnished an unfortunate example for the proprietary colonies.

The defeat of the three expeditions sent against the French resulted in the breakdown of the whole British plan of offensive operations. The border was in greater danger of attack than after Washington's defeat in 1754. At that time the war still retained much of the clandestine character of its early stages, and the French hesitated to move against the region east of the Alleghanies, an area indisputably England's. The French were not strong and, in possession of the disputed territory, were content with defensive tactics. Braddock's expedition changed the whole situation. The support of the expedition by the British government, the presence of British regiments, and the attacks against other French points took away what was left of the covert nature of the struggle. Strengthened by reinforcements, emboldened by their defeat of Braddock, and with access to the English settlements over the Braddock road, the French became aggressive, the offensive passed into their hands and the colonies were compelled in self-defense to give more adequate support to the war.

CHAPTER V

COLONIAL DEFENSE

Faced with the question of defense after Braddock's defeat, Dinwiddie took immediate measures to protect Virginia. Arms were sent to Fairfax County; the militia of the three frontier counties of Hampshire, Frederick, and Augusta was called out; that of the nine contiguous counties was ordered ready for service.[1] Fearing that the success of the French might inspire hopes of freedom in the Negroes, steps were taken to prevent a slave uprising.[2] Dinwiddie called an extra session of the assembly for August.

While Dinwiddie prepared for local defense, he advocated another attack on Fort Duquesne in letters to Colonel Dunbar, Braddock's successor, Colonel Innes, of the Virginia forces, George Washington, of Braddock's staff, and to governors Sharpe, Morris, and Shirley.[3] His recommendations were without effect. A military council decided that the morale of the troops would not permit another effort.[4] The British regiments retired to Philadelphia, whence they went into quarters at Oswego and Albany. The Virginia forces were stationed at Cumberland on their own frontier, but the men, badly

[1] *Dinwiddie Correspondence,* II, 98, 99, 101, 110.

[2] *Ibid.,* II, 102–3, 114.

[3] *Ibid.,* II, 118–19, 122, 123, 126, 127–28, 130.

[4] *Sharpe Correspondence,* I, 264–65.

demoralized by defeat, deserted until the troops were practically useless.[5] They certainly were no great obstacle to the French and Indians. The first occasional attacks of the summer were considered by the frontier people as the forerunners of wholesale destruction, and the border people prepared to move back to the more populous districts.[6] The deplorable situation on the frontier supplied the needed motive of self-preservation to awaken Virginia to action.

Defense was the main question before the assembly when it met in August, and dominated all its acts. Even Dinwiddie was willing to accept purely defensive measures, though he still cherished his idea of an offensive and insisted that the only true defense was the expulsion of the French from the Ohio.[7] He called the attention of the burgesses to the country's greater liability to attack by reason of the newly opened Braddock road. For the colony's defense he asked men, money, scalp bounties, and laws for the reorganization of the militia.[8] The burgesses, under the stimulus of threatened raids, gave his requests for defense measures a support never accorded his offensive policy. They accepted practically all of his recommendations except his idea of an offensive as the best defense, an idea seemingly unfeasible at this time.

The most important defense measure was the act

[5] *Dinwiddie Correspondence*, II, 163, 210, 233; *Sharpe Correspondence*, I, 273, 284.

[6] *Dinwiddie Correspondence*, II, 100, 132, 153, 154, 155, 210-11; *Sharpe Correspondence*, I, 251, 267, 272, 273, 367-68.

[7] *Journals of Virginia House of Burgesses*, 1752-55, p. 297.

[8] *Ibid.*, 1752-55, p. 298.

appropriating £40,000 paper to support an army of
1,200 men to be raised by voluntary enlistment. If this
method were unsuccessful after a three months' trial,
the governor could draft the required number from the
militia.[9] The act did not bear equally on all classes. The
poor could not avoid service, but the more well-to-do
were able to, for the draft section provided that service
could be commuted by payment of £10 to be used for
military purposes.[10] Even with this opportunity to buy
exemption the act was the strongest measure yet voted
by the colony. It provided for a small army and money
sufficient to maintain it until the next regular session of
the assembly.

The army, the first line of defense, was supplemented by the militia, which, because of its very nature,
was unreliable. The burgesses recognized the advisabil-
ity of reforming this force, and passed measures to improve it. The militia act of 1738 was replaced by a new
law designed to secure better attendance at musters,
more adequate arming, and more thorough military
training.[11] The burgesses also tried to secure stricter
discipline in the militia by strengthening the penal
clauses of the act of 1748 on invasions and insurrections. Graduated penalties ranging from small fines to
the death sentence were established.[12] The law was improved but subsequent events proved it still insufficient
for a proper control of the militia. In an attempt to
eliminate the Indian menace a bounty of £10 per head
was placed upon the scalps of all hostile male Indians

[9] Hening, *Statutes*, VI, 521–30.

[10] *Ibid.*, VI, 527.   [11] *Ibid.*, VI, 530–44.   [12] *Ibid.*, VI, 544–50.

above the age of ten years.[13] With the passage of this act Virginia's important war measures for this session were complete.

Though the burgesses recognized the necessity of defending the border, they did not hesitate to embody in the defense acts the usual safeguards against the misuse of executive power. The appropriation measure provided for the customary committee on expenditures.[14] The militia act and the law for the regulation of the militia when in service were limited to two years.[15] The militia could be used only in the colony's settled areas.[16] In spite of these checks, the governor's capacity to defend the frontier was now considerably increased.

The assembly passed the measures for defense in the face of bad economic conditions. Drouth extending over practically all of Virginia decreased seriously the production of corn and tobacco. The curtailment of these two staples meant a very great lessening in economic resources.[17]

When this situation is considered in connection with the known opposition of the colony to the war in its first stages, the stimulus given the burgesses by the needs of defense is evident. Appeals by the governor to their loyal support of British aims had had no appreciable effect. The burgesses saw the colony ruined by a grant of over £10,000 when they were asked to aid Braddock and the border was not threatened. But when confronted with his defeat and the murderous raids of the enemy

[13] *Ibid.*, VI, 550–52.

[14] *Ibid.*, VI, 524–25.

[15] *Ibid.*, VI, 544, 550.

[16] *Ibid.*, VI, 548.

[17] *Writings of Washington*, I, 157.

in the summer, ruin did not fall on the province by a vote of £40,000 paper, 1,200 men, and the remodeling of the militia.

Maryland and Pennsylvania were equally in danger, but although Virginia unhindered by constitutional disputes could act with energy, her neighbors permitted contests between governors and legislatures over questions of the proprietors' prerogatives to defeat all protective measures. Governor Morris, meeting his legislature in the last of July, asked for a militia and money for the purchase of arms and ammunition.[18] To secure favorable action, Morris announced a proprietary grant of lands west of the Alleghanies, free of quitrents for 15 years, to the colony's troops.[19] The legislature dallied over the governor's requests and made the impossible proposition that Morris have Colonel Dunbar's British army protect the frontier.[20] Then the house voted £50,000 in bills of credit to be raised by a tax on all real and personal property.[21] Morris changed the bill to exempt the proprietor's estates.[22] The house adhered to its measure, and the governor rejected it.[23] The request for a militia was also refused.[24]

But the legislature was not wholly opposed to protective measures. It had proposed the use of Dunbar's army, and when the frontier asked for aid, voted by resolve £1,000 for the "King's use,"—the defense of the

[18] *Pennsylvania Votes of Assembly*, IV, 415–16.

[19] *Ibid.*, IV, 418.

[20] *Ibid.*

[21] *Ibid.*, IV, 418–19.

[22] *Ibid.*, IV, 421–22.

[23] *Ibid.*, IV, 450–51, 452.

[24] *Ibid.*, IV, 453–54.

frontier.[25] Evidently all of the opposition to Morris' proposals did not come from Quaker aversion to war. A group of Quakers and non-Quakers opposed the proprietors because the Penn prerogatives limited local self-government and permitted the Penns to escape burdens borne by the colonists. This faction used the appropriation act to place the Penns in an awkward position. The proprietors were given the choice of having their real property taxed by the people or of bearing the opprobrium of refusing their part in provincial defense. The offer of Morris to grant lands free of quitrents was an attempt to minimize in England the charge of neglecting the frontier's defense by showing that the Penns were willing to do their part.[26] When the legislature met again in September the dispute of the previous session was continued. A deadlock ensued and defeated all protective measures for the frontier,[27] which in a short time was to be harried from one end to the other by French and Indians.

In Maryland Governor Sharpe, thinking that he could expect no favorable action from his delegates until Pennsylvania set a better example, refused even to summon his assembly.[28] As he had no appropriations for an army, Sharpe tried to protect the frontier by a small body of troops maintained by popular subscription,[29]

[25] *Ibid.*, IV, 455; *Pennsylvania Archives, 1st ser.*, II, 392.

[26] *Pa. Col. Recs.*, VI, 518.

[27] *Ibid.*, VI, 617–23, 624–37.

[28] *Sharpe Correspondence*, I, 262–63; *Pennsylvania Archives, 1st ser.*, II, 397.

[29] *Sharpe Correspondence*, I, 252, 367, 368.

but found his plan opposed by the delegates. They argued that if the governor could raise money for public purposes, assemblies would be useless and government would be operated by executive orders.[30] During the remainder of the year Sharpe continued to raise and support troops by popular subscription, despite this protest, and although Maryland's border suffered from raids,[31] he persisted in refusing to call the assembly because he thought a meeting would be useless until the proprietor had made concessions on the question of licenses.

The only other colony of the southern group to consider the question of supplies was North Carolina. Governor Dobbs secured £9,000 paper money to maintain 150 men placed unreservedly under the control of the commander-in-chief in America. This money, like the earlier appropriation of £8,000 paper, was granted from the £18,000 paper left unissued in the appropriation measure of 1754.[32] The source of the money and the people's need for a greater medium of exchange[33] indicate that the motive of the grant, as in 1754, was a desire to increase the amount of money in circulation rather than the need of defense. The colony was distant from the Ohio danger region, with Virginia intervening. It had allowed the unrestricted use of its troops, an unusual permission, which would not have been granted had it been seriously menaced.

[30] *Ibid.*, I, 251. [31] *Pa. Col. Recs.*, VI, 643–44.

[32] *North Carolina Records*, XXIII, 422–23; V, 333, 439–40, 573; C. J. Bullock, *The Monetary History of the United States*, p. 160.

[33] *North Carolina Records*, V, 573, 595.

North Carolina's acts in addition to Virginia's defense provisions were the only measures taken by the central and southern groups of colonies to guard against French and Indian raids. They left Governor Sharpe with no available forces for defense. Second in command to Governor Shirley, who succeeded Braddock, he was responsible for the southern colonies. His own colony had given him no troops; Virginia's forces were restricted to their own borders; and those of North Carolina were too few to be a real factor. As a result, co-operation between the colonies was impossible, and each was compelled to care for its own defense as best it could.

The means taken by Virginia to defend her borders proved inadequate. Raids begun shortly after Braddock's defeat increased in number and destructiveness as the season wore on. By September marauding parties made many Augusta County people leave their farms.[34] Raiders struck the border near Cumberland, advanced toward Winchester, and terrorized the whole northwestern frontier.[35] Washington, in charge of frontier defense, found the militia rebellious and useless even under the new laws for its discipline.[36] The colony was compelled to rely solely upon the regular troops to meet enemy raids. The assembly's provision for raising troops by volunteering and by draft was only indifferently suc-

[34] *Dinwiddie Correspondence*, II, 153, 154, 184–85, 198–99, 210, 218–19.

[35] *Letters to Washington*, I, 103–4; *Writings of Washington*, I, 192, 193, 196.

[36] *Dinwiddie Correspondence*, II, 237.

cessful.[37] Dinwiddie, evidently distrustful of the people's attitude toward the war, was intimidated by resistance to the draft in the tidewater area,[38] and as the measure was usable at his option, refused to employ it further.[39] This made volunteering the sole means of securing troops. But even with defense foremost there was no general enthusiasm for the war, and the people refused to enlist in any numbers.[40] By December only one-half of the proposed 1,200 men had been raised.[41]

The effectiveness of Virginia's little force was almost destroyed by abuses which resulted largely from opposition to the war and the continued inadequacy of the laws for military discipline. Desertion, harboring of deserters, disorder, and insubordination remained uncorrected evils.[42] It was evident that if Virginia were to maintain her frontier, more stringent laws for controlling the troops were needed. To secure such legislation Dinwiddie summoned an assembly.

When it convened in October Dinwiddie asked for stricter military laws. He also presented Shirley's request for the appointment of commissioners to attend a meeting at New York to concert measures against the

---

[37] *Letters to Washington*, I, 100–101, 143; *Dinwiddie Correspondence*, II, 307; *Writings of Washington*, I, 210.

[38] *Dinwiddie Correspondence*, II, 201; *Writings of Washington*, I, 208.

[39] *Dinwiddie Correspondence*, II, 307; *Letters to Washington*, I, 100–101, 143.

[40] *Letters to Washington*, I, 100–101, 143.

[41] *Dinwiddie Correspondence*, II, 307.

[42] *Writings of Washington*, I, 195–96; *Dinwiddie Correspondence*, II, 237.

French, and he requested a law giving scalp bounties not only to whites but to friendly Indians.[43] The burgesses, influenced by economic depression and defense expenses, refused to send commissioners to the New York meeting.[44] The proposals relating directly to Virginia's defense received a more favorable answer. In an effort to make the army more efficient the assembly passed a rigid military law for its control. It provided the death penalty for desertion and other major offenses, offered rewards for the apprehension of deserters, and established punishments for all who sheltered them.[45] Although the measure was not wholly satisfactory, it was an improvement. The proposal to win Indian allies by scalp-bounty payments was also accepted by the burgesses.[46]

They then turned their attention to economic conditions, which continued to be adversely affected by crop failure. A short crop had increased tobacco prices. People who had contracted obligations in tobacco were thus compelled to pay an augmented debt. In response to the demands of the debtors that a fair price be established at which tobacco debts might be paid, the assembly passed an act which made such debts payable in money at a certain rate per hundred pounds of tobacco for a year.[47] The burgesses ventured upon further experiments in finance. Paper money voted in the two previous sessions had circulated practically on a par

---

[43] *Journals of Virginia House of Burgesses*, 1752–55, pp. 319–20.

[44] *Ibid.*, 1752–55, p. 321.　　　　[46] *Ibid.*, VI, 564–65.

[45] Hening, *Statutes*, VI, 559–64.　　[47] *Ibid.*, VI, 568–69.

with silver and gold,[48] and this evidently encouraged the
house to try the experiment on a larger scale. A bill for
creating a land office issuing £200,000 paper money for
eight years with little security was introduced.[49] It was
a measure contrary to Dinwiddie's royal instructions,
and so displeasing to him[50] that he ended the whole question by dissolving the house.[51]

Although the burgesses had gone astray on the paper
money question, they had given the colony a measure
for securing active Indian aid and a law for the army's
discipline patterned after that of England but not so
stringent. The latter act included the usual checks for
safeguarding the rights of the citizen. The duration of
the law was limited to one year. A soldier accused of an
offense against military law was entitled to trial by
court-martial. This tribunal was to sit within definite
hours, and its sentences had to await the governor's confirmation.[52] Although these checks limited the powers
of the military authorities, the act provided sufficient
control over the troops to make possible an effective
army.

In two previous sessions the house had refused to
give this necessary authority, although the need for it
was evident. Only great danger, the devastated frontier,

[48] *Dinwiddie Correspondence*, II, 172.

[49] *Writings of Washington*, I, 206–7; *Journals of Virginia House of
Burgesses*, 1752–55, pp. 328, 330.

[50] *Writings of Washington*, I, 206–7; *Dinwiddie Correspondence*,
II, 277.

[51] *Dinwiddie Correspondence*, II, 263.

[52] Hening, *Statutes*, VI, 560–64.

and the growing conviction of the burgesses that the military law was inadequate made the assembly pass a stricter act for discipline and place Virginia's citizens when drawn into service at the disposal of the military authorities. The assembly, slow to support Braddock in an offensive campaign, when the colony was on the defensive and faced with raids was prompt to vote money and to reorganize the militia. More destructive raids and the collapse of the defense made the burgesses waive a part of the rights of the citizens, give the military greater power, and attempt the building of a more effective army. This action was taken despite the examples set by Pennsylvania and Maryland.

But these two colonies in turn were eventually to be dominated by defense needs. A devastated frontier accomplished in Pennsylvania what governor's instructions, neighbors' appeals, proclamations of free lands, pleas of loyalty to the Crown's western policy, and even the likelihood of destructive raids after Braddock's defeat could not do. In October and November the Susquehanna region was attacked,[53] and Governor Morris immediately called a legislature to provide defense for the frontier. An army, laws for its discipline, and money were needed. The supply bill precipitated a quarrel between the governor and representatives over the legislature's right to tax the proprietary estates.[54] During the deadlock Indians were ravaging the frontier and peti-

---

[53] *Pa. Col. Recs.*, VI, 645, 646, 671, 673–74.

[54] *Pennsylvania Archives, 1st ser.*, II, 447; *Pennsylvania Votes of Assembly*, IV, 495–96, 497, 504–5, 506–7.

tions for measures of defense came in from various parts of the colony.[55] Citizens of Chester asked the house to discontinue unnecessary disputes with the governor.[56] The mayor, aldermen, and council of Philadelphia remonstrated that the purpose of the session was supplies and a militia law.[57] Philadelphia was affected through the great increase in her poor caused by the invasion of refugees from the border. The frontier people made threats against the assembly.[58]

On the other hand Governor Morris wrote of the assembly's position, "The People as usual are much with them. . . . ."[59] Pressure for defense finally became so great that the proprietors made a free gift of £5,000 in the hope that the house would recede from its position. The move had the desired effect, and the house omitted the taxation of the proprietor's estates from the supply bill, which was then accepted by the governor. Sixty thousand pounds, including the proprietor's gift, were voted for defense.[60] Also an act which to a degree reflected Quaker opposition to war was passed for the formation of a militia. The measure provided for voluntary enrolment and the election of officers. The officers were to draw up rules of discipline binding on the volun-

[55] *Pennsylvania Votes of Assembly*, IV, 493, 494, 495, 496, 499, 502-3, 504.

[56] *Ibid.*, IV, 495.

[57] *Ibid.*, IV, 519-20.

[58] *Pa. Col. Recs.*, VI, 667, 729.

[59] *Pennsylvania Archives*, 1st ser., II, 447.

[60] *Pennsylvania Votes of Assembly*, IV, 526; *Pennsylvania Archives*, 1st ser., II, 530-31.

teers when signed by them.[61] Morris accepted the measure, though he characterized it as "senseless," "partial," and "impracticable."[62]

Through the money grant Pennsylvania could defend her border, and a line of forts and blockhouses garrisoned by militia was erected along the frontier at strategic points from the Delaware river to the Maryland line.[63] No provision was made for co-operation with the other colonies, not even with Virginia, the only other colony near the Ohio danger area that had definitely decided on a defensive campaign.

While the central and southern colonies were occupied with protecting their frontiers, a meeting of colonial commissioners, called at Shirley's request, was held in New York, December, 1755. This conference, to which Virginia had refused to send representatives, considered measures for the conquest of Canada. The council, under the influence of the northern colonies, decided that the main attacks should be on Crown Point and the posts on Lake Ontario rather than on Fort Duquesne. Pennsylvania, Maryland, and Virginia were to furnish men for an attack on Fort Duquesne, but only after their definite quotas for the northern expeditions were filled.[64] Also the colonies south of Pennsylvania were to secure aid from the southern Indians.[65]

[61] *Pennsylvania Votes of Assembly*, IV, 516.

[62] *Pennsylvania Archives*, 1st ser., II, 531.

[63] Root, *Pennsylvania and Great Britain*, p. 308; *Pennsylvania Archives*, 1st ser., II, 560-61.

[64] *Pa. Col. Recs.*, VII, 24-29; *Sharpe Correspondence*, I, 332.

[65] *Pa. Col. Recs.*, VII, 29-31; *Sharpe Correspondence*, I, 321.

The council's recommendation concerning Indian aid fitted in perfectly with Dinwiddie's plans. In November he had instructed Peyton Randolph and William Byrd to obtain an alliance with the southern Indians for an expedition against the French in the spring.[66] Late in December Dobbs, of North Carolina, appointed representatives to act with Virginia.[67] The Indians promised their assistance and in return asked the English to build a fort in the Cherokee territory for protection against the common enemy.[68] Dinwiddie and Dobbs acted independently of the New York conference, but apparently gained what the council wished. Glen was not consulted because he had already shown an unwillingness to have any other colony making alliances with the Indians on South Carolina's borders.[69] But without his co-operation the stability of the treaty was doubtful, for Indian trade lay with his colony rather than with Virginia and North Carolina.

The remainder of the council's plan of campaign was not favored by the governors of the southern colonies. Dinwiddie, strongly desirous of an attack on Fort Duquesne, saw no chances for its reduction if his colony had first to raise forces for the northern expeditions. He declared the plan impracticable. Virginia could not raise 1,750 men, her quota, for the New York expedition, when she had been unable to raise 1,000 men in

[66] *Dinwiddie Correspondence*, II, 263, 283.

[67] *Ibid.*, II, 305; *North Carolina Records*, V, 560.

[68] *Sharpe Correspondence*, I, 338.

[69] *Pennsylvania Archives, 1st ser.*, II, 536; C. O. 5. 375, Letter of Governor Glen to B.T., April 14, 1756.

four months' time for her own defense.[70] Sharpe, the leader of the Ohio project, also had little faith in its success if the central and southern colonies had to divide their forces.[71] Nevertheless both governors placed the plan before their assemblies.

The Pennsylvania assembly convened first, in February. Although there were sporadic raids on the border, the colony determined to depend on the defense voted in the fall and refused to consider favorably either the Shirley plan or any other war measures.[72] But by April, with the defense still not functioning properly,[73] the assembly, again in session, passed a military law similar to that of Virginia.[74] This measure provided for a force of regular troops, and the colony no longer had to rely solely upon the militia for protection.

The Maryland assembly met February 23, shortly after the opening of Pennsylvania's February session. Again it had the recalcitrant example which Sharpe always supposed his assembly was only too prone to follow. So far disputes between governor and house had precluded any effective war measures, and Maryland's only protection had been Sharpe's contribution scheme and her own geographic position. Lying between Virginia and Pennsylvania and having only a short frontier, Maryland received some benefit from the defenses of

---

[70] *Dinwiddie Correspondence*, II, 328, 334.

[71] *Sharpe Correspondence*, I, 350, 351–52.

[72] *Pa. Col. Recs.*, VII, 18–64.

[73] *Pennsylvania Archives*, 1st ser., II, 574–75; *Pa. Col. Recs.*, VII, 77, 98, 99, 120–21.

[74] *Pa. Col. Recs.*, VII, 73, 92, 125.

her neighbors. But in the fall of 1755 and the spring of 1756 these were penetrated and Sharpe's measures were inadequate. Her borders suffered only slightly less than those of Virginia and Pennsylvania.[75] Demands for lands near the frontier fell off. In the spring, 1756, Sharpe estimated that the losses in rent from the abandonment of land would be £1,600.[76] This loss made the proprietor instruct Sharpe to concede the proprietor's claim to the disputed license fees in the hope that the assembly would appropriate money for defense.

This concession, together with the devastated frontier, had more effect on the assembly than Pennsylvania's refusal to grant aid in the February session. After working on a supply bill for 12 weeks a measure for £40,000 paper money was passed. Of this amount £25,000 were provided for a western expedition in case the other colonies should attempt one, and the remainder of the fund was voted for specific measures of defense. No appropriations were made for the New York expeditions.[77]

In the last of March the assembly of Virginia met, after that of Maryland had been in session for a month. Maryland's delay and Pennsylvania's denial of a grant in February were unfortunate examples for the Virginia burgesses. A second factor tending to make them hesitant to vote additional aid for military measures was the poor economic condition of the colony. This situation had carried over from 1755 and was reflected in petitions sent to the house. Hampshire County asked exemption

---

[75] *Sharpe Correspondence*, I, 287, 409-10.

[76] *Ibid.*, I, 294, 399.

[77] *Ibid.*, I, 383, 415, 424.

from taxes because the crops there had been destroyed by Indian raids.[78] Freeholders and merchants of Caroline County represented that they could not support their families and pay war taxes because of crop failures and the scarcity of cash.[79] Goochland, Hanover, Henrico, Chesterfield, and Charles City called the attention of the burgesses to their economic difficulties and asked the establishment of a loan office and the issuance of paper to the amount of £300,000 or more as a relief from their embarrassments.[80] A bill for a loan office was introduced into the house, but did not go beyond a second reading.[81] Although the colony's economic troubles were not great enough to induce the burgesses to enter upon the hazardous experiment of a loan office, undoubtedly the power of the people to pay taxes had lessened since the spring session of 1755.

Dinwiddie laid before the assembly the plans of the New York conference, but they were given no support by the burgesses.[82] The session was dominated by the needs of defense. All during the spring, before and while the burgesses were meeting, word came repeatedly to Williamsburg of raids of the enemy and the inability of the provincial forces to protect the hinterland.[83] The

[78] *Journals of Virginia House of Burgesses,* 1756–58, p. 364.

[79] *Ibid.,* 1756–58, pp. 338–40.

[80] *Ibid.,* 1756–58, p. 357.

[81] *Ibid.,* 1756–58, pp. 372, 383, 384–85, 386, 394.

[82] *Ibid.,* 1756–58, pp. 336, 345, 350.

[83] *Virginia Magazine of History and Biography,* XIX, 292–304; *Dinwiddie Correspondence,* II, 382–83; *Writings of Washington,* I, 234–35, 241–42, 248–50.

border near the Potomac west of the Blue Ridge suffered severely. Many families abandoned their homes.[84] The people of the northern counties east of the Blue Ridge, although not actually raided, became terrified and prepared to move from the danger area.[85] People west of the Blue Ridge held meetings to discuss capitulating to the French.[86] The danger reached its height in April, 1756, when the French and Indians defeated a detachment of the Virginia regiment and penetrated almost to Winchester.[87] The whole colony was alarmed, believing that the piedmont district was threatened. Dinwiddie called out one-half the militia of the eleven counties near the menaced territory. The "Gentlemen Associators," a company of one hundred horsemen led by Peyton Randolph, the attorney-general, proposed to march with two hundred volunteers to Winchester's aid. The proposed expedition was unnecessary, for the attack was merely a raid which was soon turned back.[88] The French incursions were made by small parties operating in the north near the upper Potomac, and were directed at widely separated points, making it almost impossible for Vir-

[84] Letter of Reverend James Maury to Philip Ludwell, 1756, on "Defense of the Frontiers of Virginia," *Virginia Magazine of History and Biography*, XIX, 292–304; *Writings of Washington*, I, 234–35, 264, 265.

[85] Letter of Reverend James Maury to Philip Ludwell, 1756, on "Defense of the Frontiers of Virginia," *Virginia Magazine of History and Biography*, XIX, 292–304.

[86] *Writings of Washington*, I, 254.

[87] *Sharpe Correspondence*, I, 391.

[88] *Letters to Washington*, I, 239; *Dinwiddie Correspondence*, II, 411.

ginia's small forces to stop them. As a result the Virginia settlements were driven back to the Blue Ridge.

The defense of the frontier was further handicapped by the same circumstances which helped to render it futile in the summer and fall of 1755. The frontier people still refused to do anything.[89] The militia continued to be of little use. The regular forces, poorly trained and few in numbers, were unable to protect the long border. Even the governor failed in the emergency. Poor judgment in the appointment of subordinates to Washington, delay in carrying out measures for defense voted by the assembly, lack of scrutiny of administrative details, and want of courage in the enforcement of the draft law marked Dinwiddie's conduct of the defense.[90] With no military training, he persisted in interfering with Washington, who had been placed in charge of Virginia's forces at the time of Braddock's expedition.[91]

Executive interference caused disorder and uncertainty in the administration of defense and did much to render it inept. The failure of Governor, people, militia, and regular forces to meet the danger created a serious situation, yet the burgesses delayed action,[92] perhaps influenced by the poor economic condition of the colony, the example of her neighbors, and the determination of

[89] *Writings of Washington*, I, 241–42.

[90] *Ibid.*, I, 200–201, 208; *Dinwiddie Correspondence*, II, 82, 177.

[91] *Writings of Washington*, I, 278–79.

[92] William Fairfax to Washington, Williamsburg, April 26, 1756: "The Proceedings below Stairs go on slowly notwithstanding on hearing of the many and repeated Invasions of our Enemies, They appear alarmd and are for imeadiate Dispatch. Yet a few Hours lull their Fears and all's well again" (*Letters to Washington*, I, 230–32).

the commander-in-chief to direct the main expedition to the north. It was not until the report of the Winchester attack that the assembly acted. Washington's letters reporting the attack to Dinwiddie are dated April 19 and 22.[93] A bill providing for an army and forts was passed April 24.

The colony granted 1,500 men and £25,000 paper money. Two thousand pounds of this sum was to be spent in the erection of forts from Great Cape–Capon River in the north to the south fork of the Mayo River in the south. The army was to be raised by volunteering, but the law provided that in case the required troops were not secured within a given time the remaining numbers might be conscripted from the militia.[94] The people hated the draft, but the assembly was forced to use it by the failure of other means.[95] The draft provision was much like that of 1755, which had failed because Dinwiddie feared to employ it, but differed from its predecessor, for it was mandatory upon the governor if the required troops had not been secured within a given time.

The French and Indian raid, which had helped force through the army bill, also influenced the assembly to strengthen the militia. An amendment to the acts on invasions and insurrections was introduced on April 23

[93] Washington to Dinwiddie, April 19, 22, 1756, *Writings of Washington,* I, 247–48, 248–51.

[94] Hening, *Statutes,* VII, 13, 14–15, 18.

[95] Langdon Carter to Washington, Williamsburg, April, 1756: "Should we talk of Oblying men to serve y Country y° are sure to have a fellow mumble over ye words Liberty & Property a thousand times" (*Letters to Washington,* I, 236).

and passed on May 3, just 10 days after its introduction.[96] The act provided for the appointment of commissioners who were to provision the militia. Thirty thousand pounds paper money were appropriated for the militia's support when called into service.[97] All of the war measures placed greater powers in the governor's hands, but his increased authority was hedged about with restrictions to prevent its abuse. The act providing an army and money for its support contained the usual checks. The troops were to serve for a definite period of time.[98] Their radius of action was restricted to the settled limits of the colony.[99] The appropriation was in the hands of a committee of the house.[100] The burgesses insisted on a voice in the defense by requiring the governor to establish the line of frontier posts.[101] Also the militia act contained a limitation because the measure was an amendment to the law of 1755, which would expire in less than two years' time.[102] These checks did not unduly hamper the military forces, but they did restrict the colony's efforts to defensive measures.

Besides strengthening the regiment and militia, the colony tried to reinforce its alliances with the southern Indians. Dinwiddie placed before the house the agreement which he and Governor Dobbs had made in the winter with the Cherokees. The burgesses approved it

[96] *Journals of Virginia House of Burgesses*, 1756–58, pp. 381, 384, 386, 393, 394.

[97] Hening, *Statutes*, VII, 30, 32. [100] *Ibid.*, VII, 13.

[98] *Ibid.*, VII, 15–16. [101] *Ibid.*, VII, 17–18.

[99] *Ibid.*, VII, 17. [102] *Ibid.*, VI, 544–50; VII, 26.

and resolved that a fort should be built in the Cherokee territory out of the money Dinwiddie had received from England.[103] Dinwiddie agreed to the resolution, set aside £800 for the fort, and asked the house to appoint commissioners to estimate the cost and to supervise the erection of the post.[104] The house complied with the governor's request and agreed to furnish £2,000 paper money to cover any additional expense over and above the governor's £800.[105]

The assembly also attempted to guard against enemies within the province. When the Acadians had been dispersed throughout the colonies, over 1,100 had been sent to Virginia. Dinwiddie described them as "bigotted Papists, lazy and of a contentious Behav'r,"[106] and the colonists, influenced by their nationality, religion, and possible intrigues with the Negroes, considered them a menace.[107] The sentiment increased with the increasing fear of the French and intensified the religious prejudice already roused by the war. The suspicion against all Catholics culminated at this time in a law requiring members of that faith who refused to take the oaths prescribed by Parliament to have their names recorded at court and forbidding them to keep arms except by the court's permission.[108] The house solved the Acadian

[103] *Journals of Virginia House of Burgesses*, 1756–58, p. 368.

[104] *Ibid.*, 1756–58, p. 370.

[105] *Ibid.*, 1756–58, p. 372.

[106] *Dinwiddie Correspondence*, II, 306.

[107] *Ibid.*, II, 286; C. O. 5. 52, Secret Correspondence, March 19, 1756.

[108] Hening, *Statutes*, VII, 35–39.

problem by setting aside £5,000 paper money to pay their transportation to England.[109]

The defensive measures of the session formulated under French pressure were an improvement over previous acts. The colony's protection was henceforth the army and a strengthened militia. The regular troops were stationed in the frontier forts, ready in case of raids to go to the aid of the local militia, which was to hold the enemy in check until the arrival of a superior force. Although this plan did not prevent hostile raids, it was followed until the successful attack on Fort Duquesne.

The decisions of Virginia and Pennsylvania to pursue defensive measures only effectively nullified Maryland's conditional vote for a western expedition. All three colonies refused to comply with Shirley's plan of campaign. Their refusal was due not only to the dominance of local needs of defense, but also to the subordination of the western frontier to the northern. Perhaps the greatest need in 1756 for unity of action by the colonies was leadership of sufficient insight to plan a general campaign which would take cognizance of the particularistic feelings of each colony and direct its energies to the field in which it was most concerned. Such leadership continued to be a missing quantity through the years of 1756 and 1757, the period of Loudoun.

[109] *Journals of Virginia House of Burgesses,* 1756–58, pp. 345, 370; Hening, *Statutes,* VI, 39–40.

CHAPTER VI

THE PERIOD OF LOUDOUN

The Earl of Loudoun was appointed governor of Virginia and commander-in-chief of all the North American forces, March, 1756. This was one of England's moves for a more active prosecution of hostilities. A formal declaration of war was seen to be imminent and came May, 1756. A new plan was made for Indian affairs, which had again been conducted by the governors after the death of Braddock. Control was placed in two Indian agents appointed by the Crown, rather than in the commander-in-chief as provided in 1755. These agents were to manage only political relations with the Indians; commercial affairs, as formerly, were left in the hands of the separate governors.[1] Two districts were formed: the northern included Pennsylvania and the colonies north; the southern, Maryland and the colonies south. Sir William Johnson and Edmund Atkins were appointed agents for the northern and southern districts, respectively. This arrangement, in force for the rest of the war, was designed to secure united action on the western front in all political matters connected with Indian relations.

The British plan for aggressive action against France in America included the strengthening of the British forces in the colonies. In addition to other troops,[2] the

[1] Beer, *British Colonial Policy*, p. 254.

[2] J. W. Fortescue, *History of the British Army*, II, 296.

government sent two skeleton regiments to the colonies and asked that they be raised to full strength. These troops were named the Royal Americans. To raise them quickly it was decided to allow the enrolment of white indentured servants, a class especially numerous in the central and southern colonies. An act of Parliament permitted their enlistment in the regiments, but unfortunately furnished no means of reimbursing the masters suffering loss. This obligation was left to the colonial assemblies.[3]

Loudoun and his troops did not arrive in America until the latter part of July. The commander-in-chief decided that the British offensive should be directed against Ticonderoga while defensive operations should be pursued on other colonial fronts. Loudoun's late arrival and his subordination of the Ohio district to the northern area diminished greatly whatever chances there were for aid from Pennsylvania and the southern colonies.[4] He asked the governors for men and supplies, and, like Braddock, particularly requested that the grants be made to a general fund which should be at his disposal.[5]

His requests were only partly complied with by the central and southern colonies. The year 1756 was one of defense on the Ohio front for both sides. English offensive operations were directed to the north. The Eng-

[3] *Sharpe Correspondence*, I, 467, 472; *Writings of Washington*, I, 298-99, 300; *Dinwiddie Correspondence*, II, 480, 514; Hening, *Statutes*, VII, 61-63.

[4] *Dinwiddie Correspondence*, II, 447, 448, 449.

[5] *Journals of Virginia House of Burgesses*, 1756-58, p. 402.

lish threat in the north and their post at Oswego on the French line of communications between Quebec and Fort Duquesne prevented the French from reinforcing their Ohio post. Aid for Fort Duquesne could be sent only from the feeble Mississippi settlements. Until after the capture of Oswego and the English defeat in the north, the French on the Ohio were insecure and sent out only a few parties to raid the English borders. Thus there was little pressure to force the colonial assemblies to act, and the lack of this compelling force permitted local considerations in many cases to dominate imperial needs.

In Pennsylvania defense had been improved by the establishment of a regular army. Raids cut through the border, but they were not frequent, and the governor and assembly did not feel a great need of furnishing additional defense for the frontier. Both parties stood firmly by their positions on constitutional questions; Quaker opposition to war was active; and no favorable answer was made in the early summer to Loudoun's request.[6] The destruction of Fort Granville the last of July did not greatly alter matters, for the attack was sporadic and was not followed at once by further destruction on the frontier.[7]

In September the situation changed. The assembly heard of the fall of Oswego, which gave the French control of the Great Lakes, made their line of communications on the western frontier secure, and possibly presaged severe attacks on the English border. Money had

---

[6] *Pennsylvania Votes of Assembly*, IV, 581, 582, 583.

[7] *Ibid.*, IV, 584–85, 587, 589, 595, 603.

to be voted, as the available funds for maintaining defense were exhausted.[8] The necessity of safeguarding the frontier again dominated constitutional questions. Even Quaker principles became quiescent. The governor and house compromised their constitutional differences and agreed on a measure for £30,000 paper to be redeemed in ten years.[9] The house refrained from insisting on a part in the expenditure of the appropriation and allowed the governor a free hand in the disposal of the money for purposes of defense.[10] The governor accepted the ten-year redemption period, although the proprietors usually opposed issues of paper for long periods of time.[11] The grant was sufficient to maintain the defense for the rest of the year.

During this period Pennsylvania waged war upon the hostile Delawares of the Susquehanna and Cayuga country.[12] The Indians were severely punished and made peace at Easton, November, 1756.[13] The treaty freed Pennsylvania's border from this enemy, and during the fall lessened the pressure upon the authorities for aid.

Much of the Pennsylvania assembly's recalcitrancy in the war had been attributed to Quaker control of the house, but this disappeared in 1756. The situation in Pennsylvania during the fall of 1755 had aroused the authorities in England, and it was proposed in 1756 that Quakers should be excluded from the assembly by im-

[8] *Pa. Col. Recs.*, VII, 229.

[9] *Ibid.*, VII, 264.   [10] *Ibid.*, VII, 256.

[11] *Ibid; Pennsylvania Votes of Assembly*, IV, 284.

[12] *Pa. Col. Recs.*, VII, 88–90.   [13] *Ibid.*, VII, 257–63, 313–38.

posing an oath on all representatives by act of Parliament. A measure to this end was introduced into Parliament, but prominent London Quakers promised to persuade the colonial Friends not to stand for re-election, and the bill was withdrawn. A number of Quakers resigned from the assembly; others refused to stand for election when a new house was chosen in the fall;[14] and when the assembly met in October, Quaker domination was gone.[15] Despite the removal of this element there was no great enthusiasm for the war, and the struggle over constitutional questions continued to interfere with complete participation in the conflict.

The summer sessions of Pennsylvania's assembly foreshadowed the course of Maryland. The situation in the Baltimore proprietary was much like that in Pennsylvania. Contests over constitutional questions dominated unless the demand for protection was very great. French inactivity and her neighbors' defenses made her short border fairly free of raids during the summer. The needs of defense were not pressing enough to force the quarrel between governor and assembly into the background. The Maryland people were influenced further against support of the war by the loss of many of their indentured servants, who had taken advantage of the parliamentary act permitting their enlistment in the Royal Americans. Threats were made against the recruiting officers, and mobs attempted to take away their recruits.[16]

[14] Root, *Pennsylvania and Great Britain*, pp. 311–12.

[15] *Pennsylvania Votes of Assembly*, IV, 626.

[16] *Sharpe Correspondence*, I, 461, 462.

Under these conditions the Maryland delegates met in September, 1756. No additional money for war purposes had to be voted, as there were still funds left from the £40,000 paper granted in the spring. The assembly maintained the existing defense and voted money to indemnify masters whose servants had been taken for the army. Small sums were appropriated for the royal forces in New York and for securing recruits for the Royal Americans.[17] These appropriations for the general service were made probably because of the pressure felt in all the colonies by Montcalm's destruction of Oswego. Sharpe could not induce his burgesses to comply further with Loudoun's requests, and in disgust prorogued the house.[18]

The answers returned to Loudoun by Pennsylvania and Maryland were paralleled somewhat by Virginia's. Dinwiddie, in placing Loudoun's requests before the September session, especially recommended Loudoun's plan of having all appropriations made to a general fund,[19] a proposal rejected by the burgesses, who persisted in maintaining a voice in the expenditure of money. Under little pressure from raids[20] and feeling reasonably secure with an army of six hundred men, seven hundred militia, and three companies of rangers on the frontier,[21] the assembly voted no additional money for the border's protection. Only specific appropria-

[17] *Ibid.*, I, 494, 495.
[18] *Ibid.*, I, 495.
[19] *Journals of Virginia House of Burgesses*, 1756–58, p. 402.
[20] *Writings of Washington*, I, 341.
[21] *Dinwiddie Correspondence*, II, 474.

tions were granted from existing funds. Eight thousand pounds paper were voted to raise men for the Royal Americans and to reimburse masters whose servants might enlist.[22] Virginia, like the other colonies, made this grant for the general service probably because of French success at Oswego.[23] Two other specific grants provided funds for strengthening the colony's position with the Indians, £2,000 to garrison the Cherokee fort, £3,000 to pay Indians for assistance against the French.[24] The three specific grants totaled the war measures of this session and showed the colony willing to stand on its untested defense provisions of the spring.

Despite its satisfaction with these measures they were not adequate. Defects in the military system militated against its success. The officers of the militia in the several counties were generally elected by the men and had little control over them.[25] Each county's militia, in violation of the militia law, operated only within its own environs.[26] This custom threw the main burden of defense on the sparsely populated area, the region most exposed and least able to sustain it. Gradually the practice became established that a particular detachment of militia served for one month at a time.[27] When its period ended the militia left, regardless of the safety of the

---

[22] Hening, *Statutes*, VII, 61–62, 63.

[23] *Journals of Virginia House of Burgesses*, 1756–58, p. 402.

[24] Hening, *Statutes*, VII, 62–63.

[25] *Dinwiddie Correspondence*, II, 504, 528–29, 569.

[26] Hening, *Statutes*, VI, 113; VII, 14, 107; *Writings of Washington*, I, 331.

[27] *Writings of Washington*, I, 374–76.

local inhabitants.[28] That body evidently did much as it pleased, and certainly was not an effective unit in border defense.[29]

The inefficiency of the militia had its counterpart in that of the ranger companies. When the companies were formed their ranks were not recruited to the full numbers provided by law. Promises made to the men were not fulfilled, and in a short time desertions became frequent. By the last of September, 1756, the number of the rangers was so reduced that their work was taken over in great part by the regiment.[30]

The unsatisfactory situation found in the militia and rangers also prevailed in the colonial regiment. Volunteering failed as before to secure the required troops,[31] and the draft likewise was unsuccessful.[32] By August, four months before the date set by law for the expiration of the service, but six hundred of one thousand, two hundred men had been secured by voluntary enlistment and draft.[33]

This force made up Virginia's army during the fall and winter of 1756–57. Dinwiddie, as the head of Virginia's military forces, kept Washington in command of the regiment. Unfortunately the governor continued to interfere in the border's defense, and at times wholly

[28] *Ibid.*, I, 357.

[29] *Dinwiddie Correspondence*, II, 474, 504, 528.

[30] *Writings of Washington*, I, 353, 378–79.

[31] *Dinwiddie Correspondence*, II, 442.

[32] *Writings of Washington*, I, 298–99; *Dinwiddie Correspondence*, II, 447, 480, 506.

[33] *Dinwiddie Correspondence*, II, 474.

disregarded Washington's advice; approved of his plans
one day and reject them the next. In despair over the
continual interference, Washington wrote:

Whence it arises, or why, I am truly ignorant; but my strongest representations of matters relative to the peace of the frontiers
are disregarded as idle and frivolous; my propositions and measures, as partial and selfish; and all my sincerest endeavours for the
service of my country perverted to the worst purposes. My orders
are dark, doubtful, and uncertain; *today approved, tomorrow con-
demned.* Left to act and proceed at hazard, accountable for the
consequences, and blamed without benefit of defence. . . . .[34]

Dinwiddie began to consult wholly with Loudoun, and
drew away from Washington, neglecting to inform him
of his plans until he began to feel ". . . . entirely like
a Wanderer in unknown paths."[35]

The lack of co-operation between governor and
commander of the regiment, together with the unstable
character of the military forces, made the defense in-
effective, and in the late fall the French and Indians
raided the upper Potomac district. The population of
Augusta, Frederick, and Hampshire counties again began to flee toward the Carolinas.[36] Winter alone gave
the harried settlements respite from raids.

Though the year's operations had resulted in failure
for the colonies, the future held hope, for changes were
taking place in the ministry. In November, 1756, William Pitt came into the cabinet as secretary of state for
the southern department and began preparations for a
more active prosecution of the war. The colonies were

[34] *Writings of Washington,* I, 404.
[35] *Ibid.,* I, 352.
[36] *Ibid.,* I, 360–61; 377–78; *Sharpe Correspondence,* I, 492.

divided into two military districts: the northern composed of New England, New York, and New Jersey, the southern of Pennsylvania and the colonies to the south. Each colony was asked to provide troops both for its own defense and for the general service, while troops and a fleet were to be sent to America for operations against the French.[37]

In spite of the preparations for a more vigorous campaign, results in 1757 were attended with failure. Pitt was not in complete control, and the incompetent Loudoun was still in command. In February, at a conference of colonial governors at Philadelphia, Loudoun outlined his plan of a great offensive against Louisburg and defensive measures for the southern colonies. Five companies of the Royal Americans were sent to South Carolina, supposedly in danger of French attack, and to this force the other southern colonies were to add definite quotas of troops. The protection of the western border near the Ohio was intrusted to Pennsylvania, Maryland, and Virginia, aided by five companies of the Royal Americans to be stationed on the Maryland-Pennsylvania frontier.[38] Loudoun's ideas for carrying out Pitt's orders for a strong campaign placed on the southern colonies the dual task of participating in an offensive movement far from their own borders and at the same time caring for their own defense. In the case

[37] G. S. Kimball, editor, *Correspondence of William Pitt When Secretary of State with Colonial Governors and Military and Naval Commanders in America*, I, 5–6; *Pennsylvania Archives, 1st ser.,* III, 96–97.

[38] *Sharpe Correspondence,* I, 533; *North Carolina Records,* V, 750–52.

of both campaigns of 1756, directed by Shirley and Loudoun through New York, the southern colonies had
shown their unwillingness to take part in expeditions
which did not immediately concern their own borders.
Loudoun's proposed attack in 1757 on the extreme eastern flank of the French had still less likelihood of securing aid from the southern colonies. Even their support
of the conference's defensive plans depended greatly on
the power of the French threat.

The first answer to the conference came from Pennsylvania, where the assembly had been in session through
practically the entire winter. Although there had been
few raids on the frontier, defense had to be maintained
to meet the constant danger of attack. By the last of
December, 1756, the funds for supporting the provincial
forces were exhausted.[39] The need of continuing the existing defense was the principal pressure on both governor and assembly to force their agreement on supply
measures. Although both parties knew that money had
to be provided, they quarreled over the appropriation
measure until March, 1757, when a money bill exempt-
ing the proprietor's estates from taxation but assigning
the troops to definite duty and placing the funds in the
hands of a committee selected by the assembly was offered the governor.[40] The measure violated Denny's
instructions, but on pressure from Loudoun, who acted
on Dinwiddie's advice, he accepted it.[41] The act pro-

[39] *Pa. Col. Recs.*, VII, 441.

[40] *Pennsylvania Votes of Assembly*, IV, 703, 704; Root, *Pennsylvania and Great Britain*, pp. 313–14.

[41] *Pitt Correspondence*, I, 41; *Pennsylvania Archives*, 1st ser.,
III, 99.

vided £100,000 paper to raise and support 1,400 men. No troops were granted either for Loudoun's expedition or for South Carolina.[42] The assembly's chief concern was, not the broader aspect of the war, but the local border's protection, which now consisted of a system of forts, 1,400 men, money to support them, and detachments of the Royal Americans.

With frontier defense provided, and in the absence of raids, both governor and house insisted upon the utmost limits of their respective claims. Loudoun's requests for additional troops, laws for forming a militia and for regulating Indian affairs were defeated.[43] Twice the colony participated in intercolonial defense. In June the assembly by law permitted the governor to send two hundred troops to South Carolina,[44] a measure accepted by the governor although he considered that he, as commander of the colony's forces, had sole control of the troops.[45] Probably the motive of the house was to force his acknowledgment of its power over the provincial forces. In August, 1757, Montcalm took Fort William Henry and threatened New York with invasion. The Pennsylvania assembly, in session at the time, felt the French pressure and immediately reacted by empowering the governor to send one thousand men to aid New York.[46] The French success had no effect on the south-

[42] Root, *Pennsylvania and Great Britain*, pp. 313–14.

[43] *Pennsylvania Archives, 1st ser.*, III, 195; *Pennsylvania Votes of Assembly*, IV, 721, 745–47, 750, 760; *Pa. Col. Recs.*, VII, 464.

[44] *Pennsylvania Votes of Assembly*, IV, 719.

[45] *Pa. Col. Recs.*, VII, 563, 575, 578, 582.

[46] *Pennsylvania Votes of Assembly*, IV, 732.

ern colonies, for the French withdrew before their assemblies met. It may be that an additional factor influencing the Pennsylvania house to make a grant of men for New York was the opportunity of again asserting its control over military affairs.[47]

In March, 1757, while the Pennsylvania assembly was holding its first session, the Maryland assembly met. The funds for defense were not yet expended and the border had hardly suffered at all from raids.[48] However, the menace of the French was always present, and the term of service for the Maryland forces was about to expire. These two factors exercised whatever pressure there was to force the governor and assembly to agree. The assembly voted forces neither for Loudoun nor South Carolina, but passed one measure of defense providing for a small number of men.[49] Like previous measures, the act specifically stated what could be done with the troops[50] and placed the expenditure of the appropriation granted from the original £40,000 measure of 1756 under the control of the agents of the house.[51] It was accepted by Sharpe, though he disliked to have his military powers curtailed.[52]

The money maintained the defense until September, 1757, when exhaustion of the funds required another session of the assembly. With pressure on the border slight and the defense strengthened by the stationing of

[47] See note 45, p. 117.

[48] *Pitt Correspondence*, I, 10-11.

[49] *Sharpe Correspondence*, II, 3.

[50] *Ibid.*

[51] *Ibid.*, II, 51-52.

[52] *Ibid.*, II, 16-17.

five hundred Royal Americans on the western frontier,[53] both governor and delegates could insist stubbornly on their claims to power. The immediate cause of dispute was Fort Cumberland, located on Maryland's southern edge, far from her settlements, and benefiting only Virginia. Sharpe's insistence that Maryland send forces to the fort antagonized the delegates, who resolved not to give supplies to any Maryland company stationed there.[54] The supply bill offered by the house reduced the forces for the frontier's defense and definitely limited them to patrolling the border and garrisoning Fort Frederick, Maryland's strongest post on the frontier.[55]

To secure a more favorable measure, appeal was made to Loudoun, who was tactless and did not understand American assemblies. For the consumption of the delegates he wrote Sharpe:

I do demand from the Province of Maryland that the 500 men furnished for the Crown Cause, and Employed by me this Last Summer, in the defence of their Garrisons on their Frontiers be Continued in the Service this Winter, as absolutely necessary for the Defence of their own Province, and the Defence of His Majesty's Dominions. —— As to their Disposing of the Troops in the Winter I have the King's Commission to Command all men that are or shall be in Arms in North America; I am on the Spot, and whilst the King does me the Honour to Continue that Commission to me I will Execute it, and if any Officer or Soldier presumes to disobey my orders, I will treat him as the Law directs.[56]

Sharpe, dominated by a regard for the superiority of everything British, transmitted the letters to the house

[53] See above, p. 115.   [54] *Sharpe Correspondence*, I, 91.
[55] *Pitt Correspondence*, I, 121–23.
[56] *Sharpe Correspondence*, II, 97.

in the hope of influencing it, but the letters only made the delegates more hostile. They laid taxes on the estates of the proprietor as well as the colonists'; the troops were placed under agents of the house: and it was stipulated that no orders whatever from the Earl of Loudoun were to be obeyed.[57] Both governor and house refused to recede from their positions, and no measure for defense was passed.[58]

While the Maryland assembly had not been influenced appreciably by the rumored attack on South Carolina, North Carolina, close to the supposed French objective, voted funds in May, 1757, to send two hundred men to that colony.[59] To protect North Carolina's southern frontier, Governor Dobbs ordered two-thirds of the militia from the four southern counties to be ready for service.[60] During the summer it became evident that South Carolina was not to be attacked, and the effect of the lessening of outside pressure was seen in the fall session of the assembly. When funds for the troops were exhausted in November, money was appropriated to maintain forces for a year, but the number of men was reduced from three hundred to one hundred and fifty.[61]

[57] *Ibid.*, II, 107–8.

[58] *Ibid.*, II, 109.

[59] *North Carolina Records*, V, 846, 848; XXV, 345.

[60] *Ibid.*, V, 763; C. O. 5. 297, letter of Governor Dobbs to B. T., May 30, 1757.

[61] *Pitt Correspondence*, I, 154; *North Carolina Records*, XXV, 350–52; C. O. 5. 375, letter of Governor Lyttleton to B. T., July 12, 1757.

South Carolina, down to 1757, had taken almost no
part in the war. Her course, dictated by her jealous
guarding of her Indian trade, had been largely obstruc-
tive. The threatened French attack made South Carolina's assembly vote £26,000 sterling and seven hundred
troops—two hundred for defense and five hundred for
general service. During the year the colony granted in
all £48,900.[62] The stimulus to action, danger from the
enemy, was the same in South Carolina as in the other
colonies. A mere rumor of French attack aroused her assembly to wonderful exertions.

The pressure from the French threat which moved
the other colonies to action during the spring likewise
affected Virginia. There were few raids on the border
during the winter and spring, but the colony remembered the ineffectiveness of its defense in the fall. The
regiment, the colony's main reliance for protection, was
in wretched condition.[63] Virginians, reviewing the colony's course in the war, could see only one failure after
another in the attempts to protect the border. When the
assembly met in April, 1757, the time was ripe for
changes. War appropriations were exhausted, measures
for control of both militia and the army were about to
end, the French were threatening to establish themselves south of Virginia in South Carolina, and the colony might have to meet the enemy not only in the West,
but in the South. Virginia, like Pennsylvania and Maryland, was dominated by necessity of safeguarding the

[62] *Pitt Correspondence*, I, 86–87; C. O. 5. 421, "South Carolina
Acts," July 6, 1757.

[63] *Letters to Washington*, II, 45–47.

frontier, and no supplies of men or money were granted for Loudoun's Louisburg expedition. A measure for defense was passed which appropriated £80,000 paper money for various war purposes.[64] Of this amount £10,-000 were to take the place of paper money issued in 1755 and 1756 but now called in.[65] Seventy thousand pounds were devoted to direct war purposes, of which £25,000 were to extinguish the debt arrears of pay due the regiment, the rangers, and the militia. Six thousand pounds were designated for 300 rangers and £3,000 for Indian aid.[66] Thirty-six thousand pounds were alloted for raising and maintaining the regiment.[67] In all, including the rangers, approximately 1,600 men were voted.[68]

The regiment was to be raised by a draft administered by a court in each county composed of the county justices and the chief officers of the militia,[69] with power to impress into service all men with no occupations, those who had deserted their wives and children, "all other vagrant and dissolute persons not having lawful means of employment," and all who had received the £10 bounty for enlistment under the last draft act and had deserted before the expiration of their service.[70] In case a county's quota was not filled by these selected individuals, drafts were to be made from the militia. After the draft the county might resort to voluntary en-

[64] Hening, *Statutes*, VII, 81.

[65] *Ibid.*, VII, 81–82.

[66] *Ibid.*, VII, 76.

[67] *Letters to Washington*, II, 87–89.

[68] Hening, *Statutes*, VII, 70, 76.

[69] *Ibid.*, VII, 69–71.   [70] *Ibid.*, VII, 70.

listment to fill its quota.[71] Seven companies of the troops
were specified for Virginia's frontier, one for the Cherokee fort, and two for South Carolina. Two companies
to be raised after the others were also to be sent to South
Carolina if the commander-in-chief thought necessary.[72]

After designating the placement of the troops the
house made no further effort to take part in the conduct
of campaign. Earlier appropriation measures had provided a house committee which with the governor determined how the money should be spent. This committee was now abandoned, although it had given the
house an important part in military affairs. Perhaps
the burgesses realized that their committee divided
military authority and made it impossible to place the
responsibility for failure where it properly belonged.
The house limited the power of its committee to examin-
ing and settling the accounts of the men in service.[73]

The appropriation act furnishing men and troops
had to be supplemented by an act providing for control
of the troops. Washington's request for a stricter law,[74]
the failure of the old law, and the type of men to be
drafted resulted in the passage of a stringent mutiny and
desertion act. A law practically like that of England's
was enacted for one year.[75]

The assembly's legislation included measures for a
militia and laws for its regulation. The expiration of
the old laws gave the burgesses a chance to make a more

[71] *Ibid.*, VII, 70–71, 72.   [72] *Ibid.*, VII, 75.

[73] *Writings of Washington*, I, 441; Hening, *Statutes*, VII, 75.

[74] *Writings of Washington*, I, 436–41.

[75] Hening, *Statutes*, VIII, 87–92; *Letters to Washington*, II, 65–69.

effective weapon of this force, but they failed to grasp
the opportunity and continued the former measures
with a few minor changes for limited periods.[76] Provisions for securing Indian aid were strengthened. The
bounty on the scalps of hostile Indians was raised from
£10 to £30.[77] The Virginians were especially desirous
of bringing the southern Indians into the war, for since
the beginning of 1757 there had been rumors that the
French were working among the Cherokees and under-
mining English influence with them.[78] To block the
French, keep the Indians friendly, and secure their aid,
Virginia engaged officially in the southern Indian trade
and by law provided a board of factors known as the
"Trustees of the Indian Factory of Virginia," giving it
full power over the Indian trade and voting it £3,000
paper money to purchase goods for the trade. The trustees were to contract with individual traders, and furs
and skins received were to be sold to English merchants.[79] The act was to endure for five years, but the
scheme was actually abandoned in 1760 when the Cherokees became hostile.[80] Although Virginia may have had
designs on the southern fur trade, the chief object of
the measure was to keep the Indians friendly and to enlist their aid. The provisions to secure Indian assistance
completed the defensive program.

[76] Hening, *Statutes*, VII, 93–106, 106–16.

[77] *Ibid.*, VII, 121–23.

[78] *Dinwiddie Correspondence*, II, 449–50, 451, 539–40; Hening,
Statutes, VII, 116.

[79] Hening, *Statutes*, VII, 116, 117, 118.

[80] *Ibid.*, VII, 354–55.

The assembly's legislation was influenced by an absence of pressure from actual raids on the one hand, the continual threat of possible invasion, the expiration of old defense laws, and the rumored attack on South Carolina, on the other, and resulted in a compromise. The increased appropriations for war, the concentration of military power in the hands of the executive, and the drastic mutiny and desertion law were advances in protective measures. The refusal to improve the militia and the establishment of an army of vicious classes were the weaknesses of the assembly's work. The summer and fall were to witness the breakdown of its war measures. Because of illness and engrossed in preparations for a departure to England, Dinwiddie gave little attention to administrative affairs.[81] The soldiers went unpaid; the draft was not successful; the men forced into service were practically uncontrollable and deserted in large numbers.[82] The authorities had little success in preventing desertions, and during the summer the army simply dwindled away.[83] In the late fall, when the troops were thoroughly discouraged, the border was raided. Once more the frontier was in confusion, the inhabitants pushed back to the piedmont, and anew it was demonstrated that the conquest of the French points on the Ohio was necessary for the frontier's safety.

Virginia had pursued defensive measures since Brad-

[81] *Journals of Virginia House of Burgesses*, 1756–57, p. 414; *Letters to Washington*, II, 151, 204, 225, 230.

[82] *Letters to Washington*, II, 130–31, 226–28; *Dinwiddie Correspondence*, II, 584–85, 677; *Sharpe Correspondence*, II, 59, 79.

[83] *Sharpe Correspondence*, II, 79.

dock's defeat in 1755, showing an interest solely in the defense of its own borders. No part had been taken in the offensives of 1756 and 1757 because they had no direct connection with the danger immediately threatening the colony, but the disasters from 1755 to 1757 compelled a recognition of the futility of purely defensive measures. Safety demanded that the French be driven from the Ohio,[84] and to make that possible, colonial forces, an able governor, and encouraging aid both of men and money from England were necessary. The lessons gained from bitter and costly experiences, the tact shown by the new governor, Francis Fauquier, the efficiency displayed by Pitt, the subsidies furnished by Parliament, the restoration of Fort Duquesne to a position of importance in operations against the French, supplied the forces necessary to make Virginia a factor in the war.

[84] *Dinwiddie Correspondence*, II, 455–56, 547; *Writings of Washington*, I, 256–58; *Letters to Washington*, II, 115, 229–30; *Pitt Correspondence*, I, 289–90.

CHAPTER VII

THE YEAR OF VICTORY

The year of victory, 1758, saw Pitt in complete control of Great Britain's war tactics. As secretary of state he was primarily responsible for the colonies and for international diplomacy. He also kept his hand on the military and naval services, thus helping to insure co-operation between them. His conduct of the war had both European and world aspects. He kept France busy in Europe by furnishing subsidies to his ally, Prussia. His plan for America contemplated a concerted attack on the French. The plan appealed directly to the self-interest of the colonies. The northern colonies, threatened by the French along the northern and northeastern border, were to support the campaigns against the center and eastern flank; the southern colonies, endangered by the French on their western border, were to aid forces commanded by General Forbes in an attack on Fort Duquesne. Pitt, in a spirited circular letter, asked the colonies to raise men for these purposes and attempted to insure colonial support for the war by promising to have the Crown pay for all arms and provisions and to ask Parliament to grant the provinces a proper compensation for their aid. This was merely a continuation of Parliament's old policy of subsidies.[1]

The colonies had every reason to co-operate in the British plan. Although there were few actual raids on

[1] *Pitt Correspondence*, I, 136–51.

the frontier, the colonists knew that as long as the French held the Ohio there was danger of such attacks, for three years of experience had made apparent the futility of merely defensive methods. A British and colonial expedition against Fort Duquesne recognized the immediate interests of the southern colonies and gave them a real opportunity to secure permanently a safe frontier. In addition the assemblies of the southern colonies had evidence that Pitt's promise of asking Parliament to reimburse them for their expenditures meant something, for Parliament in 1757 had granted them £50,000 sterling in return for their war grants.

In Pennsylvania Pitt's plan received delayed approval from the assembly, which met in March. The house quickly voted to raise 2,750 men, but the appropriation measure contained a clause taxing the proprietor's estates. The governor objected to this provision, and speedy action was blocked. Not until April 22, only eight days before the troops were expected to be ready, did the governor and house compromise their dispute in an appropriation measure of the same tenor as that of 1757.[2]

Grants, which were only delayed in Pennsylvania, were completely blocked in Maryland by a similar struggle. Governor Sharpe and the house were at odds over control of the troops and taxation of the proprietor's estates.[3] When the assembly met in April to answer

---

[2] *Pennsylvania Votes of Assembly,* IV, 794–95, 799, 804, 805–6, 811, 814–16, 817, 818–19; *Pitt Correspondence,* I, 230.

[3] *Sharpe Correspondence,* II, 104–5, 109, 125, 133, 135, 138–39, 146–47, 149.

Pitt's requests, both governor and house were too. blinded by their quarrel to seize the opportunity of safeguarding the colony from future French attacks. Compromise was impossible and Maryland refused to aid.[4]

Pitt's requests met with a prompt response from Virginia, where no contest between governor and house for power obstructed action, and the proposal to attack Fort Duquesne was popular. The acting governor, John Blair, reported that the plan was favored in Virginia. Governor Dinwiddie, Washington, John Robinson, speaker of the house, Richard Bland, and John Baylor, burgesses of prominence, had all recommended the capture of the Ohio forks as a good defensive measure.[5] Virginia was also encouraged by the allotment to her of over £32,000 of the £50,000 granted by Parliament in 1757.[6] The assembly met in March and quickly voted 2,500 men and £32,000 paper money for war purposes.[7] The troops were designated for specific services, three hundred rangers for frontier defense, two thousand men for the Ohio expedition.[8] The Ohio troops were to be secured by maintaining the first regiment and by raising a second which was to continue in service until December 1, 1758.[9] Frontier defense was strengthened by em-

[4] *Ibid.*, II, 168–69, 177, 244.

[5] *Pitt Correspondence*, I, 289; *Dinwiddie Correspondence*, II, 650–51; *Writings of Washington*, I, 256–58; *Letters to Washington*, I, 386–95; II, 115, 229–30.

[6] Beer, *British Colonial Policy*, p. 55; Hening, *Statutes*, VII, 372–73.

[7] Hening, *Statutes*, VII, 163–65, 166–67.

[8] *Ibid.*, VII, 163–65.   [9] *Ibid.*, VII, 168.

powering the governor to draft militia for garrisons in the border forts until December 20, 1758.[10]

In April, after Virginia's splendid answer to Pitt's requests, the North Carolina assembly was held. Here also was no acrimonious dispute between governor and house; Virginia's recent grants doubtless had a favorable influence; and North Carolina too had shared in Parliament's £50,000 grant of 1757. In fact there was nothing to prevent the colony from giving such aid as its strength would permit, and in eight days £7,000 paper money was voted to maintain three hundred men for the western attack.[11] Before June 22, two hundred of these troops were at Alexandria on their way to join the expedition against Fort Duquesne.[12]

North Carolina was the third of the southern group of colonies to give a favorable response to Pitt's requests. South Carolina, the fifth colony of this division, like Maryland, made no grants for the Forbes expedition. In an exposed position she was probably too weak to do more than defend herself.[13]

The heartiest response to Pitt from the southern colonies was given by Virginia with a grant of money, two regiments, three companies of rangers, and drafts from the militia. The regiments were raised by voluntary enlistment stimulated by a bounty.[14] To raise them

[10] *Ibid.*, VII, 169.

[11] *Pitt Correspondence*, I, 240; *North Carolina Records*, V, 934–35.

[12] *Sharpe Correspondence*, II, 209; *Pitt Correspondence*, I, 240, 279.

[13] *Pitt Correspondence*, I, 310–11; C. O. 5. 474, "South Carolina Commons House Journal," January 18, March, 18, 1758.

[14] Hening, *Statutes*, VII, 164.

quickly captains' commissions were granted to the first
responsible individuals recruiting companies of fifty
men.[15] The measures were successful, and the troops
were ready by June 5 to leave for the general rendez-
vous.[16] The raising of Virginia troops was the climax of
the colony's war ardor; but enthusiasm soon subsided,
largely because of dissatisfaction with the management
of the campaign. General Forbes's success was dependent upon colonial support, and this was contingent upon
the colonies' faith in his disinterestedness and his ability
to succeed. Virginia's confidence in him weakened during the summer, when opinion developed that Forbes
was partial to Pennsylvania. He had landed in Philadelphia, established his headquarters there, and from
the beginning was surrounded by Pennsylvanians, who,
gaining his ear, had given him his first impressions of
colonial conditions and had used their opportunities for
their own benefit.[17]

Their great chance came in the choice of the road
the army should follow to attack Fort Duquesne. Two
routes were considered: a new trail entirely within Penn-

[15] *Pitt Correspondence*, I, 289-90.

[16] D. Brymner, editor, *Report on Canadian Archives*, Bouquet Collection, p. 76; *Pitt Correspondence*, I, 275-76.

[17] John Armstrong, commanding the Pennsylvania regiment, to
Richard Peters, secretary of the colony, Raystown, October 3, 1758:
"The Virginians are much chagrin'd at the Opening of the Road thro'
this Government & Colonel Washington has been a good deal Sanguine
& Obstinate upon the Occasion but the presence of the General has
been of great Use on this as on Other Accounts; . . . . Colonel B——t
is a very sensible & Useful Man, notwithstanding, had not the General
come up, the Consequence wou'd have been dangerous" (*Pennsylvania
Archives, 1st ser.*, III, 552).

sylvania, and the Braddock road leading from Virginia. The Braddock road had been carefully made, but not having been used during the three years the colonies were on the defensive, had become overgrown and needed brushing out, which required only a small amount of time and labor. In 1759 Alexander Finnie with thirty workmen in sixteen days put the road in condition to permit a train of sixty provision wagons, five hundred sheep, and seventy head of cattle to pass over it into Pittsburgh.[18]

The Pennsylvania trail was shorter, led from a more thickly settled area where supplies could be obtained more easily for the army, but required the construction of an entirely new road from Raystown on. Forbes chose the Pennsylvania road, since known by his name.

The decision of Forbes almost alienated the Virginia groups most influential in spurring the colony on to support the war. One group included those interested in the Ohio Company and other persons who believed the future prosperity of the province lay in the West. They wanted the expedition to go through their colony, make Virginia the center of military operations, open up roads to the frontier and thence to the West, and give Virginia a dominant position in Indian trade and western lands. The choice of the Forbes road meant the defeat of these aims. A second group was engrossed with the purpose of ending the war. These people supported the expedition because it promised victory. They considered Forbes's decision for a new road the result of Pennsylvania influ-

[18] *Journals of Virginia House of Burgesses*, 1758-61, p. 139.

ences[19] and thought it would cause delay and jeopardize the expedition's success. Probability of failure due to such a cause materially decreased the willingness of this group to aid.[20] The cause of both the Virginia parties was in the hands of Washington and the other army officers. Washington, actuated both by his own economic prospects and the greater interests of Virginia, upheld the advantages of the Braddock road and strongly opposed the selection of the Pennsylvania route. He warned Colonel Bouquet, in command of the advance forces, that making a new road was almost sure to produce delay, which would greatly discourage Virginia.[21] When Forbes made his choice of roads Washington believed it was due to Pennsylvania influence.[22] Exasperated by the success of

[19] John Kirkpatrick, Washington's secretary, to Washington, March 19, 1759, "The Pensilvanians I suppose will reap the fruits of this Harvest—which the Virginians have Long toiled and Laboured for —I saw Plainly the Whole Campaign was favoured For them" (*Letters to Washington*, III, 154–56).

[20] Robert Rutherford to Washington, July 31, 1758: "I fear Our Country has Lavished a Large Sum for Little or no Purpose—In short there Appears so great an infatuation throughout the whole, that I have realy Lost hope of a Persons either gaining Credit or giving Sattisfaction for even this new man at the Helm, Seems to be already Prepossess'd and Certainly entertains the most inconsistent notion of the Frontiers that ever enter'd the Mind of Man" (*ibid.*, III, 3–4).

[21] *Writings of Washington*, II, 62–72.

[22] Washington to Fauquier, September 2, 1758, "The Pennsylvanians whose present as well as future interest it was to conduct the Expedition thro' their Government, and along that way, because it secures at present their frontiers and the trade hereafter—a chain of forts being erected—had prejudiced the General absolutely against this road; made him believe we were the partial people; and determined him at all events to pursue that rout" (*ibid.*, II, 91–92).

the Pennsylvanians and sure of the failure of the expedition, he wrote Speaker John Robinson:

The conduct of our leaders (if not actuated by superior orders) is tempered by something I do not care to give a name to. But I will say they are————[23] or something worse to P-j-v-n artifice, to whose selfish views I ascribe the miscarriage of this expedition; for nothing now but a *miracle* can bring this compaign to a happy issue. . . . . Can General Forbes have orders for this? Impossible. Will, then, our injured country pass by such abuses? I hope not. Rather let a full representation of the matter to his Majesty. Let him know how grossly his glory and interest, and the public money, have been prostituted. . . . . It hath long been the luckless fate of Virginia to fall a victim to the views of her crafty neighbors, and yield her finest efforts to promote their comon interest, at the expense of much blood and treasure! Whilst openess and sincerity have governed her measures.[24]

Colonel Bouquet denied that either he or Forbes were biased in the choice of routes, and charged Washington and Colonel Byrd with prejudice for the Braddock road.[25] Whatever the merits of the controversy, Forbes's choice of routes increased the active jealousy between Virginia and Pennsylvania, made for disruption rather than co-operation in the colonial forces, destroyed Virginia's confidence in the commanding officer and in the success of the undertaking.[26]

Forbes had selected the Pennsylvania route partly

[23] Blank in manuscript.

[24] *Writings of Washington*, II, 86, 87–88.

[25] Bouquet to Forbes, Raystown, July 21, 1758, *Report on Canadian Archives*, Bouquet Collection, p. 92; Forbes to Bouquet, Carlisle, July 23, 1758, *ibid.;* Forbes to Bouquet, Raystown, August 8, 1758, *ibid.*, p. 93.

[26] *Letters to Washington*, III, 94–95.

because it was shorter than the Braddock road,[27] and haste in completing his campaign was important because both Pennsylvania and Virginia troops were voted to serve only until December 1, 1758. But circumstances beyond his control made the army's progress slow. Camp equipment was delayed;[28] road-making unexpectedly difficult;[29] the provision train always lagged behind;[30] and a rainy autumn made the newly built roads almost impassable.[31] The troops left Raystown, where the real road-making began, about August 1, and did not reach Fort Duquesne until November 25, almost four months later.[32] During the summer and early fall this slow advance strengthened Virginian opinion that the unwise and prejudiced choice of roads would prevent success.

The halting progress of the expedition began by September to threaten it with defeat. Bouquet wrote Forbes from Raystown that the position of the army was critical. He described the troops as becoming dispirited, and warned Forbes that it was necessary for his reputation to act, as no explanation would be received if the

[27] *Pitt Correspondence*, I, 295.

[28] *Report on Canadian Archives*, Bouquet Collection, correspondence between Colonel Bouquet and Sir John St. Clair, May 27–July 19, 1758, pp. 76–80.

[29] *Ibid.*, Bouquet Collection, correspondence between Colonel Bouquet and Sir John St. Clair, August 12–October 15, 1758, pp. 80–82; correspondence between Colonel Bouquet and General Forbes, August 18–November 22, 1758, pp. 93–96; general correspondence of Colonel Bouquet, August 15–26, 1758, pp. 118–19.

[30] *Pitt Correspondence*, I, 373.

[31] *Ibid.*, I, 374.   [32] *Writings of Washington*, II, 116.

expedition failed.[33] Toward the last of October Forbes, despairing of taking Fort Duquesne in the fall,[34] began to make preparations for defending the frontier during the winter and launching a new expedition in the early spring.[35] Requests were made of both Virginia and Pennsylvania for troops to retrieve the fortunes of the campaign.[36]

Forbes's plan could hardly have received the support of the provinces. Virginia considered the campaign hopeless and felt that the failure of Forbes was due to his partiality for Pennsylvania. Her discouragement was further increased by the failure of the tobacco crop of 1758 because of drouth,[37] and the subsequent curtailment of the colony's resources. Slackened war interest was shown unmistakably when the Virginia assembly met in September, 1758. At first there was an inclination to discontinue all troops after December 1, 1758, the time of the expiration of their service.[38] Finally the burgesses decided on a less drastic course. The dissatisfaction with Forbes's action was so great that all support was withdrawn from the western expedition. Thus, al-

[33] *Report on Canadian Archives*, Bouquet Collection, p. 286.

[34] *Pitt Correspondence*, I, 374.

[35] *Ibid.*, I, 374-75.

[36] *Ibid.*; *Pennsylvania Votes of Assembly*, V, 2-3, 3-4; *Pa. Col. Recs.*, VIII, 224-25, 227, 229.

[37] Hening, *Statutes*, VII, 240-41.

[38] William Ramsay to Washington, October 17, 1758: "The 1st Virg^a Regim^t had like to have been broke by a Vote of the House, but the Old and Judicious, carried it against the Young Members by a Majority of five" (*Letters to Washington*, III, 117-18); C. O. 5. 1329, letter of Governor Fauquier to B. T., September 23, 1758.

though the first, Washington's regiment, was continued to May 1, 1759, it was ordered disbanded on December 1, 1758, if it had not been returned to the colonies for frontier defense by that time. The second, Byrd's regiment, was ordered discontinued on December 1, 1758.[39] All the assembly's emphasis was placed upon defense. Fifty-seven thousand pounds paper were voted for war purposes, £15,000 for the support of the troops, the rest for the payment of expenses incurred by the ranger and militia forces.[40]

The house further showed its cooling interest by the repeal of an act placing a bounty on the scalps of hostile Indians.[41] The rescinding of the law was a retrogression from Virginia's forward measures, due probably to a variety of causes. The large award for scalps had caused the development of vicious practices in which friendly as well as hostile Indians were killed, women and children murdered, and several scalps made out of one.[42] These abuses increased existing sentiment against the barbaric law. When the original measure was passed in 1755 the border was in great danger and no measure too brutal when directed against murdering savages. The situation in 1758 was changed. The border was free from raids, and a sense of security aroused a sentiment against scalp bounties strong enough to force the assembly to act. The law repealing the scalp bounty and the measures in regard to the Virginia troops comprised the

[39] Hening, *Statutes*, VII, 172.

[40] *Ibid.*, VII, 171–72, 172–73, 175, 178–79.

[41] *Ibid.*, VII, 241.

[42] *Pennsylvania Archives*, 1st ser., III, 185, 199–200.

total of the assembly's war legislation. The outstanding feature of the session was the withdrawal of the colony from offensive warfare.

The assembly had barely been prorogued when it was called again into session. Forbes, warned by Governor Fauquier and the action of the Virginia assembly that his support was weakening, proposed a quick advance upon Fort Duquesne.[43] Fauquier asked the burgesses to maintain the troops for a while longer, as they were necessary for the success of the impending attack.[44] The burgesses acquiesced and continued both regiments until January 1, 1759, in such service as the governor ordered. The men of Byrd's regiment were not obliged to serve after December 1, 1758, unless they wished.[45] This action may reflect Virginia's lack of confidence in Forbes caused by what the burgesses considered his favoritism for Pennsylvania and the slowness of his expedition. Forbes could hardly have looked upon it otherwise than a warning of Virginia's intention to discontinue her support of the expedition.

During the fall sessions of Virginia's assembly the other colonies, with the exception of South Carolina, also held meetings of their legislatures. North Carolina continued her two companies,[46] but no assistance could be expected from Maryland, where Sharpe and his as-

[43] *Journals of Virginia House of Burgesses*, 1758–60, p. 265; *Pitt Correspondence*, I, 373, 375.

[44] *Journals of Virginia House of Burgesses*, 1758–61, p. 49.

[45] Hening, *Statutes*, VII, 251–53.

[46] *North Carolina Records*, XXV, 370, 372.

sembly were still at odds over control of the troops,[47] and Pennsylvania, although benefiting greatly from the expedition, carried out the threat of Virginia and abandoned the enterprise.[48] Pennsylvania's activities were directed toward Indian relations. Money was devoted to extending her Indian trade.[49] Indian agents were appointed and goods were sent to the Indians.[50] The colony's most important transaction with them during the year was the treaty of Easton, October, 1758.[51] To appease the hostile Delaware and Shawonese Indians, Pennsylvania promised them that no settlements west of the Alleghanies would be made within the borders of their territories except with their consent.[52] This promise disregarded the claims both of the land companies and the other colonies. But the peace contributed greatly to Forbes's success. The action of the colonial assemblies determined him to make a forced march upon Fort Duquesne. He ordered a rapid advance without waiting for road-making. The French, weak in numbers and discouraged by the fall of Fort Frontenac, did not oppose the attack; the English forces entered a deserted and dismantled fort, and Virginia's hopes were at last fulfilled.

[47] *Pitt Correspondence,* I, 327–32; *Sharpe Correspondence,* II, 293–95, 297, 310.

[48] *Pennsylvania Votes of Assembly,* V, 6–7; *Pa. Col. Recs.,* VIII, 228, 229–30.

[49] *Pennsylvania Votes of Assembly,* IV, 762.

[50] *Ibid.,* V, II.

[51] *Pa. Col. Recs.,* VIII, 174–223.

[52] Alvord, *Mississippi Valley in British Politics,* I, 121.

CHAPTER VIII

WITHDRAWAL FROM WAR

The capture of Fort Duquesne had been made possible by colonial aid inspired by the wish for a safe frontier. But even with the forks of the Ohio in English control, the work of safeguarding the border was only partly done. French points on the Great Lakes dominating the Ohio country had to be taken. Indeed, if the English colonies were to be insured permanent peace, France had to be expelled from North America. This was Pitt's aim in 1759. He asked the colonies to aid by furnishing the same number of men as they had in 1758. The southern division of colonies was expected to hold the Ohio points.[1]

The Virginia assembly, meeting in February, 1759, returned the first answer to Pitt's requests. The colony felt that with the taking of Fort Duquesne its great task was done. The emergency forces were demobilized. Washington resigned his command and was succeeded by Colonel Byrd. By February, 1759, one regiment and four companies of rangers constituted the provincial forces. A part of the regiment was stationed at Fort Duquesne, renamed Fort Pitt by the English, the remainder in Virginia's frontier counties. However, the English hold on the frontier was not secure. The garrison at Fort Pitt, threatened by the French at Niagara, was in danger of being forced to retire to the Pennsylvania fron-

[1] *Pa. Col. Recs.*, VIII, 272-73; *Pitt Correspondence*, I, 417-20.

tier,[2] and such withdrawal meant the loss of everything secured in 1758. This realization moved the Virginia burgesses, and in spite of continued economic depression[3] the assembly appropriated £52,000 paper for war expenses.[4] Fifteen hundred men were to be maintained until December 1, 1759, of which 1,200 were placed unreservedly under the governor's control for general service and 300 were substituted for the rangers maintained on the frontier in the earlier years of the war.[5] Virginia's grants, although not complying completely with Pitt's requests, were generous and showed the way to the other colonies.

Pennsylvania had every reason to support Pitt's plans. English control of Fort Pitt portected her frontier. She had received undoubted benefits from having Forbes's expedition carried on wholly within her borders, had gained by the treaties of peace with the Indians, and had access to the rapidly growing Indian trade of the West by a short direct road to Fort Pitt.[6] She was planning to develop the Indian trade of her north-central territory by a road from Reading to Fort Augusta (Shamokin).[7] These considerations influenced the assembly to support Pitt's requests.

[2] *Report on Canadian Archives,* Bouquet Collection, pp. 13–14.

[3] *Journals of Virginia House of Burgesses,* 1758–61, pp. 73, 120; Hening, *Statutes,* VII, 312–14.

[4] Hening, *Statutes,* VII, 259.

[5] *Ibid.,* VII, 255–57, 279–80; *Journals of Virginia House of Burgesses,* 1758–61, p. 69.

[6] *Pennsylvania Votes of Assembly,* V, 26; *Journals of Virginia House of Burgesses,* 1758–61, p. 280, Bancroft Transcripts.

[7] *Pennsylvania Votes of Assembly,* V, 50.

The legislature, meeting in March, 1759, proposed a vote of £100,000 paper and 2,700 men. But the appropriation bill taxed proprietary estates to which Governor Denny objected, and a deadlock ensued.[8] General Amherst, commander of all the British forces in America, insisted on the governor's acceptance of the measure. Amherst's pressure and a timely gift from the representatives induced Denny to accept the appropriation measure.[9] The house won a point over the proprietor and at the same time supported the service.

This example was before the Maryland assembly when it met in April. The usual contest between governor and house prevented all aid, and Governor Sharpe, as was his wont, blamed the situation on Pennsylvania. He wrote of Governor Denny's concession to the house, "After such a Step what can the Proprietaries of Pens[a] or Gov[r] Denny expect? will they hope to preserve any Authority? or Do they not encourage the People to make any Demands on the Gov[r] & as it were tell them that if they do not want Resolution to persevere they will obtain every Thing they want be their Demands never so unreasonable."[10] Despite Sharpe's opinion that Pennsylvania's conduct affected Maryland, the influence apparently was very one-sided. There are many instances in which Maryland refused to give aid after Pennsylvania had made like refusal, but there are none when appropriations were granted by Maryland following a grant

[8] *Ibid.*, V, 30, 38, 41, 42.

[9] Root, *Pennsylvania and Great Britain,* p. 319; *Pa. Col. Recs.,* VIII, 331–32, 332–33.

[10] *Sharpe Correspondence,* II, 331.

by Pennsylvania. Indeed Maryland made but two grants of money during the entire war: one in 1754 and one in 1756. In both cases pressure on the frontier forced a temporary concession from the proprietor, which induced the house to act. Neither grant was made under Pennsylvania influence, for both were preceded by a failure on that colony's part to make an appropriation. Undoubtedly the comparative security of the border and the unwillingness of the proprietors and delegates to recede in any measurable degree from their respective positions, except when pressure was extraordinary, accounts for the absence of grants in Maryland. General Stanwix, in command at Fort Pitt, wrote, "From the Disputes arising between Governor Sharpe & The Assembly of Maryland & he not having it in his power to wave The Proprietary Instructions, as The Council in That Province are a part of the Legislature, all appointed by the Proprietor & all enjoy Places of considerable Profit by His Gift—Not a single Man is raised in this Province."[11]

Maryland's failure to vote supplies was matched by North Carolina. Down to 1759 North Carolina, with no strong incentives either to grant or refuse aid, had given an indifferent support to the war. But in the May session of the assembly the governor and house quarreled over control of North Carolina's share of the money granted to the colony by Parliament. Governor Dobbs attempted to use the funds to pay the colony's soldiers in the Forbes expedition because provincial paper money was practically worthless outside the colony's own bor-

[11] *Pitt Correspondence*, II, 133-34.

ders. The house objected to Dobbs's summary disposal
of the money and attempted to assert its control. A
supply measure was passed which also appointed an
agent in London who should be responsible to the house
and who should receive grants of money made to the
colony by Parliament.[12] The council rejected the bill
and a deadlock ensued. North Carolina's refusal to aid
Pitt and South Carolina's determination to support only
defensive measures[13] left but two colonies, Virginia and
Pennsylvania, upholding English possession of the Ohio.

During the spring and summer of 1759, the English
forces, by a series of movements in the West culminat-
ing in Sir William Johnson's capture of Fort Niagara,
removed the immediate French threat from the Ohio. In
September Quebec was captured. While the French still
held Montreal, and the Mississippi Valley, their power
was broken. Treaties in January, July, and October
with the Pennsylvania and Ohio Indians lessened the
danger of Indian attacks on the frontier.[14] Just as this
menace was being removed, trouble developed with the
Cherokees, and the pressure motive was transferred
from the western border to the south.

Hostile feeling developed between the Virginians
and the Cherokees during Forbes's campaign. The
whites of the frontier, ever contemptuous of the Indians,
attacked Cherokees who committed depredations while

[12] *Ibid.*, I, 432; II, 35, 108-9; *North Carolina Records*, VI, 34-40.

[13] *Pitt Correspondence*, II, 421-25; C. O. 5. 475, "South Carolina
Commons House Journal," July 9, 1759.

[14] *Pa. Col. Recs.*, VIII, 293-97, 383-91, 429-35.

returning through Virginia.[15] French intrigues with the Indians also aroused ill-feeling toward the English.[16] War broke out in October when Governor Lyttleton of South Carolina seized Indian chiefs in conference with him.

Just after this flare-up the Virginia assembly met in November, 1759. Governor Fauquier asked the continuance of the regiment whose term of service expired December 1, 1759, and did all he could to secure a favorable vote. He sent the house letters from North and South Carolina asking for aid against the Cherokees. He reminded the burgesses of benefits to the colony from the recently opened roads, of England's expenditure of money at Fort Pitt, and of the small amounts spent by the colony for border defense in 1759. He also advocated the completion of Fort Loudoun. This post not only protected the southwestern frontier, but served as a factory in the Cherokee Indian trade.[17] Fauquier needed to use all his tact and influence to secure a continuance of the Virginia troops, for the factors keeping Virginia in the war were rapidly losing their power. The French were no longer dangerous in the northwest, and the Cherokee question in the southwest was not yet pressing. Yet troops were needed for the posts among the Ohio Indians, who, lately allied with the enemy, were still a source of possible trouble to the English.

Fauquier's pleas were successful. The regiment was continued to May 1, 1760. Three hundred men were

[15] *Pitt Correspondence*, II, 268.

[16] *Ibid.*

[17] *Journals of Virginia House of Burgesses*, 1758–61, 133–34.

stationed on the southwestern frontier; four hundred were placed at the Crown's disposal for western service; the other three hundred could be used for the frontier's protection as the governor should command. As Fauquier would order them to act with the British troops, the Crown had seven hundred of Virginia's troops at its disposal if the colony's regiment was kept at full strength. As this was rarely done after 1758, the number must be considered as considerably under seven hundred. For the support of the regiment £10,000 were voted.[18]

The lessening pressure on the colony is evident in the supply vote. The number of men at the Crown's disposal was reduced from 1,200 to under 700; the small sum of £10,000 for the regiment's support was merely sufficient to continue that force for five months; and the troops for the southwestern border were for defensive purposes and were not meant for offensive measures against the Cherokees.

The danger from the Indians affected both North and South Carolina to a much greater degree than Virginia. Their assemblies were called into session in the fall. The North Carolina house temporarily dropped its dispute with the governor over an agent. Men and supplies were voted in both colonies and the militia ordered out.[19]

The Cherokee uprising was too distant to influence

[18] Hening, *Statutes*, VII, 332.

[19] *North Carolina Records*, VI, 60–62, 64–65, 124–25, 152; *Pitt Correspondence*, II, 184–86, 230–31; C. O. 5. 474, "South Carolina Council Journal," November 10, 1759, January 7, 1760.

the conduct of the two proprietary provinces. Maryland gave nothing; and Pennsylvania, with the French and Indian pressure lessened, felt fairly confident of her border's safety. The assembly in the December session, 1759, ordered the governor to disband all the troops except 150 men who were kept for garrison duty.[20]

In 1760 Pitt made new requests for aid.[21] No change had occurred in the French situation, but the same necessity existed for garrisoning the posts among the Ohio Indians. Pennsylvania's assembly, meeting in February, again attempted to tax proprietary estates. In the ensuing deadlock supplies were delayed until April. Governor Hamilton, who had replaced Denny, then gave way and accepted a measure similar to that of the preceding year.[22]

In March, 1760, during the Pennsylvania dispute over supplies, the Virginia assembly met. Pennsylvania's example could hardly be considered encouraging, but Virginia was more affected by the continued need of holding the Ohio posts and the Cherokee trouble. A temporary peace had been made with the southern Indians in the latter part of December, 1759, but they were discontented and at any time might become hostile. These influences secured Virginia's support for Pitt's plans. The regiment was continued from May to November, 1760,[23] but three hundred of its numbers sta-

[20] *Pennsylvania Votes of Assembly*, V, 90, 92.

[21] *Pitt Correspondence*, II, 234-37.

[22] *Pennsylvania Votes of Assembly*, V, 104, 105, 106, 107, 111-12, 113, 114; *Pitt Correspondence*, II, 276.

[23] Hening, *Statutes*, VII, 348-49.

tioned on the southwest frontier might be retained until April, 1761, if the governor so ordered. This meant that a part of the troops were voted for a longer period of time than in the preceding year.[24] For this reason more money was needed for their maintenance and the assembly appropriated £20,000 paper.[25] In brief, the measures passed merely maintained the *status quo* and so reflected the unchanged western situation.

Hardly had the house been prorogued when it was called into session again. The Cherokees, enraged at the massacre of the hostages seized by Lyttleton in 1759, were attacking Fort Loudoun.[26] The assembly appropriated £32,000 paper to raise and maintain seven hundred men until December 1, 1760. These troops, reinforced by the three hundred men stationed on the southwest border, were to relieve Fort Loudoun.[27]

South Carolina was the only colony to assist Virginia in her attempt to save her outpost. The proprietary colonies were unaffected by the uprising and North Carolina, with governor and house involved in a contest over the appointment of an agent, failed to make any grants until June 26, 1760, too late to save the fort, which had to surrender.[28] The garrison was massacred

[24] *Ibid.*, VII, 332, 348.

[25] *Ibid.*, VII, 350.

[26] *Journals of Virginia House of Burgesses*, 1758–61, p. 171; C. O. 5. 474, "South Carolina Council Journal," February 29, 1760.

[27] Hening, *Statutes*, VII, 358.

[28] *North Carolina Records*, VI, 348–62, 380, 396, 402, 437–38; *Pitt Correspondence*, II, 297–300, 316–17; *Journals of Virginia House of Burgesses*, 1758–61, pp. 289–90; C. O. 5. 299, Letter of Governor Dobbs to B. T., July 21, 1760.

on its way to Fort Prince George, in South Carolina, and the Cherokees attacked that post.[29] With its borders in danger, South Carolina's assembly met in August, voted one thousand men, of whom not more than one-half were raised, and Governor William Bull, who had replaced Lyttleton, asked North Carolina and Virginia for assistance.[30] The petition to North Carolina should have received favorable answer, for her frontier was endangered, but the assembly did not meet until November, when the contest over an agent took precedence again. The house, which had twice receded from its position in order to aid against the Cherokees, refused to do so a third time, and all grants were blocked.[31]

Virginia was confronted, not only with the Cherokee situation, but with the needs of the Ohio area as well. General Monckton, commander of the southern division, in the fall of 1760 had asked Virginia, Maryland, and Pennsylvania for troops to garrison the western posts during the winter. But with the capture of Montreal, French power in Canada had collapsed, and there was no pressure in the West to make the colonies accede to his requests,[32] for the western Indians had been inactive since the capture of Fort Duquesne. Pennsylvania and

[29] *Journals of Virginia House of Burgesses,* 1758–61, p. 289; C. O. 5. 377, letter of Governor Bull to B. T., September 9, 1760.

[30] *Pitt Correspondence,* II, 421–25; *North Carolina Records,* VI, 313–15.

[31] *North Carolina Records,* VI, 460–62, 469.

[32] September 8, Vaudreuil surrendered Montreal and signed articles of capitulation by which Canada and all its dependencies passed into English possession.

Maryland refused any appropriation,[33] and for all practical purposes withdrew from the war,[34] and Virginia, in
a session of the assembly held in November, also declined to furnish troops for the West, as she was more
concerned with her southwestern frontier.[35] The troops
at Fort Pitt were withdrawn for service against the Cherokees, and £20,000 appropriated to increase the regiment to one thousand men and to maintain it until April,
1761, the money to come from Virginia's share of the
funds granted the colonies by Parliament in 1757 and
1758.[36]

Virginia's preparations for punishing the Cherokees
fitted excellently into Pitt's plans for 1761. France was
to be driven from the Caribbean Sea and the Gulf of
Mexico; the French West Indies, the Mississippi, and
Mobile were to be attacked.[37] Punishment of the Cherokees would teach them a lesson and prevent the French
from securing savage allies to resist the English attacks
on the Mobile and Mississippi country. Regulars were
sent to South Carolina to co-operate with that colony's
troops in an attack against the lower towns of the Cherokees. Virginia was expected, while this expedition was
progressing, to raid the upper towns.[38]

[33] *Sharpe Correspondence*, II, 455, 459; *Pennsylvania Votes of Assembly*, V, 117–18, 128, 129–30.

[34] *Sharpe Correspondence*, II, 497; III, 38–39, 47–48; Root, *Pennsylvania and Great Britain*, 321–22.

[35] Hening, *Statutes*, VII, 370–71.

[36] *Journals of Virginia House of Burgesses*, 1758–61, p. 184; Hening, *Statutes*, VII, 369–72, 372–75.

[37] *Pitt Correspondence*, II, 370, 384–87, 389–90.

[38] *Journals of Virginia House of Burgesses*, 1758–61, pp. 267–70.

Virginia's assembly was called twice in 1761, once in March and again in November, to vote supplies for this purpose. The regiment in the first session was continued to December 1, and in the second to May 1, 1763.[39] In the November session the burgesses inserted a proviso in the supply act requiring the governor to disband the troops if peace was made before the expiration of the soldier's service. In all, £42,000 were voted, and again the money was to be derived from Virginia's share of Parliament's grants to the colonies.[40]

Virginia's measures for the war were accompanied by votes of men and money from North and South Carolina. South Carolina maintained the troops voted in 1760.[41] North Carolina's grants, delayed by a renewal of the contest over an agent, were made too late to be a factor in the campaign.[42] North Carolina's slowness forced Virginia to bear the whole brunt of the northern expedition against the upper Cherokee towns. The Virginia forces, impeded by natural obstacles, never reached the Cherokee country, but aided the southern expedition by constituting a threat to the upper towns. The southern expedition inflicted severe losses on the Cherokees and forced them to sue for peace. A treaty at Charleston in December, 1761, closed hostilities.[43]

When Governor Fauquier heard informally of the

[39] Hening, *Statutes,* VII, 381–82, 463–64.

[40] *Ibid.,* VII, 382, 383, 464.

[41] *Pitt Correspondence,* II, 421.

[42] *North Carolina Records,* VI, 597–98, 686–87.

[43] *Journals of Virginia House of Burgesses,* 1758–61, pp. 275, 276, 279, 297; 1761–65, p. x.

treaty he gave orders to disband the regiment.[44] Before this could be done General Amherst asked for its continuance, and Fauquier, in a January session of the assembly, put the question before the burgesses.[45] The Cherokee uprising was over, war expenses burdensome to the colony; the paper money question acute, and the people weary of war. The burgesses insisted on the provisions of the act of November, 1761, which provided troops until May 1, 1762, but required their dismissal when peace was made. When news of the formal peace was received from South Carolina the regiment was disbanded.[46]

Hardly had Virginia dismissed her troops when information came of war with Spain. Before the declaration of war the French had boasted that Spain was going to help them recover Quebec. The Family Compact of August, 1761, an offensive and defensive alliance between the Bourbon rulers of France and Spain, was another indication of Spain's entry into the war. Pitt, convinced of Spain's hostile intentions, advocated an attack upon her, and when the ministry would not support him he resigned. His successor, Lord Egremont, was forced by developments to declare war on Spain, whose possessions in America brought the war to this continent, and the colonies were again called upon to do their part.

Virginia's assembly met in March, 1762, to answer Egremont's requisitions. Spain was considered especially dangerous to the southern colonies because her pos-

[44] *Ibid.*, 1761–65, p. 33.

[45] *Ibid.*, 1761–65, p. 34.   [46] *Ibid.*, pp. 36, 47.

sessions lay near the Cherokees, but recently hostile to the English. This belief gave Virginia's waning military spirit a new impetus. Thirty thousand pounds paper were appropriated to maintain a regiment of 1,000 men until December 1, 1762, and to pay the enlistment expenses of 268 men for the British army. The troops were placed unreservedly at the governor's disposal and could be united with the British forces as the commanding general ordered.[47] The colony's forces saw no active service, for the French and Spanish powers, even when combined, were impotent. The danger from Spain was more fancied than real, and lessening outside pressure as usual was reflected in the attitude of the Virginia assembly.

In addition to the gradual decline in importance of this force, two new deterring factors were partly responsible for the cessation of all aid from Virginia. One was the formation of a new policy toward Indian lands which destroyed the hopes of colonial imperialists, the other the serious dispute with the British merchants over Virginia's paper money, which made the burgesses reluctant to spend more money in a war now removed from her borders.

It will be remembered that the imperial and colonial groups interested in western lands and trade had been unable to force their will on the British ministry, whose first cautious step toward the development of a western policy had been consent to the Ohio Company's grant in 1749. The subsequent efforts of the Ohio Company to exploit the West had been a factor in bringing

[47] Hening, *Statutes,* VII, 495–97.

on the conflict with the French, which greatly curtailed all activities in western land and trade. But with Fort Pitt in English control, the great land companies came to life and the forces of the land faction were increased by all persons entitled to land under Dinwiddie's proclamation of 1754. Among the most active members of the group were the speculators, men such as George Washington and George Mercer, who foresaw the ultimate profits to be made by land speculation.[48] The land faction's attention was focused particularly on the Ohio region, and the claims of its members included lands whose jurisdiction was in dispute between Virginia and Pennsylvania.

The two colonies, anxious to monopolize both the land and trade advantages of the West, suspiciously watched each other's moves. In 1759 a rumor that Colonel Byrd was to be placed in command at Fort Pitt alarmed members of the Pennsylvania assembly. Two of them twice waited on Governor Hamilton with this information and told him that in such an event Pennsylvania would no longer support the war.[49] In 1760 the proprietors of Pennsylvania and Maryland agreed to appoint commissioners to run the line between the two colonies.[50] Governor Fauquier received a decided impression from conversations with Pennsylvanians that in determining this line the Penns expected to gain a good amount of land supposed to be in Virginia.[51]

[48] *Letters to Washington*, III, 158–63, 163–69.

[49] *Pa. Col. Recs.*, VIII, 297–98.

[50] *Pennsylvania Archives*, 1st ser., IV, 3–36.

[51] *Journals of Virginia House of Burgesses*, 1758–61, p. 281; 1761–65, p. xiv.

Pennsylvania control of the Ohio forks with its strategic dominance of the Ohio country was not to the liking of Virginians, who feared its possible effects on 'the fur trade and the lands to which Virginia's soldiers were entitled under Dinwiddie's proclamation of 1754.[52] Virginians looked upon the West as their peculiar preserve, both because of their claims under the charter of 1609 and their colony's part in the war.[53] On the other hand Pennsylvania considered Fort Pitt within her jurisdiction and proceeded to act on that assumption.[54] Virginians, afraid of being forestalled by Pennsylvanians, put pressure on their governor to grant land patents at once in the area opened up by the French defeat.[55]

The question of land patents in the West was bound up with that of Indian affairs. In 1759 no well-developed British policy on Indian relations had yet been formulated. The Crown had made a vain effort in the Albany congress of 1754 to find a solution to the question by colonial action. The plan of the Board of Trade of the same year for colonial defense also provided for control of Indian affairs. A part of this recommendation was adopted in 1755, when the commander-in-chief of the army was given charge of political relations with the Indians. Another move was made in 1756, when north-

[52] *Ibid.*, 1758–61, p. 280, Bancroft Transcripts.

[53] *Letters to Washington*, III, 154–56, 163–69.

[54] *Journals of Virginia House of Burgesses*, 1758–61, p. 281.

[55] *Ibid.*, 1758–61,. pp. 281, 284; C. O. 5. 329, letter of Governor Fauquier to B. T., January 30, 1759.

ern and southern Indian agents were appointed and given control over political relations with the Indians.

The measures did not touch the real sources of trouble, land and trade. The abuses in land and trade and the resulting friction are depicted in letters from the Indian agents and the governors.[56] The border's defense demanded the elimination of the causes of trouble between Indians and whites. The defeat of the French and the opening of the West forced action upon the Crown, whose next step toward the formation of a definite policy was the regulation of Indian lands.

A course of action for the Crown had been pointed out by events in the colonies. It will be remembered that Pennsylvania, in the treaty of Easton, 1758, had promised the Indians that no settlements west of the Alleghanies would be made within the borders of the colony without the Indians' consent.[57] The treaty was affirmed by the British ministry,[58] and in later conferences with the Indians the promise was made repeatedly. It was affirmed at Pittsburgh, 1758, by Bouquet, commander at Fort Pitt after Forbes's departure,[59] again at Pittsburgh, 1759, by Croghan, deputy agent for the north;[60] at Pittsburgh, 1759, by Stanwix, commander of the forces of the southern division;[61] and twice at Pitts-

---

[56] *Wraxall's Abridgement, passim; New York Colonial Documents,* VII–VIII., *passim;* Alvord, *Mississippi Valley in British Politics,* I, 119–20; Beer, *British Colonial Policy,* pp. 254–55.

[57] *Pa. Col. Recs.,* VIII, 174–223.

[58] *Report on Canadian Archives,* p. 73.

[59] *Pennsylvania Archives, 1st ser.,* III, 571–74.

[60] *Pa. Col. Recs.,* VIII, 382–91.   [61] *Ibid.,* VIII, 429–35.

burgh, 1760, by General Monckton as commander of the southern division.[62]

The principle was first put into actual operation by Colonel Bouquet in 1761, when the Ohio Company was planning to establish settlements on its grant. The company proposed to settle Germans and Swiss in the country, and Bouquet was offered a share of stock to secure his influence in forwarding the company's interests.[63] Settlements meant hostile Indians, and Bouquet, in command of western defense, was more interested in a quiet border than in his own profit,[64] and refused the proposition. Later he removed squatters from the West and issued his proclamation of October 30, 1761, which forbade ". . . . any of His Majesty's subjects to Settle or Hunt to the West of the Alleghany Mountains on any Pretense Whatsoever, unless such Persons have obtained leave in Writing from the General or the Governor of their Provinces Respectively and produce the same to the Commanding Officer at Fort Pitt." Individuals violating this command were to be seized, tried by court-martial, and punished.[65] Bouquet's order asserted imperial rights in the control of the West and placed enforcement of the order in the military, a direct agent of the Crown.[66]

The course pursued by the British military officers in refusing to permit indiscriminate seizure of Indian lands was also followed by Virginia's governor when the

[62] *Pennsylvania Archives, 1st ser.*, III, 744–51, 751–52.

[63] *Report on Canadian Archives*, pp. 72, 73.

[64] *Ibid.*, p. 73.

[65] *Ibid.*   [66] *Ibid.*, pp. 74, 75.

colony's land factions made their demands on him.[67]
Governor Fauquier had a twofold position toward the
West. As the Crown's representative he was guardian of
its interests, and at the same time he had to protect those
of Virginia. Although British policy in Indian affairs
was not formulated, Fauquier may have seen in the
Crown's confirmation of the Easton treaty and the reit-
eration of the Easton principle in the Indian treaties by
the government's military officers a tendency toward
Crown control of western land. By December, 1759, he
was questioning the probability of the Crown's renewing
the grants to the Ohio and Loyal companies.[68] He proceeded cautiously on the land question, refusing to grant
any land patents in the West until he received instructions on the subject from the government.[69]

Fauquier tried to persuade the governors of Pennsylvania and Maryland to follow the same policy of refusing to grant lands in the West. He appealed to Governor Hamilton to make no grants in the Ohio region
until His Majesty's pleasure was known. He asked the
Board of Trade to have a Crown representative present
when the Maryland-Pennsylvania line was surveyed,
and requested that these colonies be enjoined from making grants in the disputed region until the line was determined.[70] Fauquier pursued the same policy toward
lands directly west of Virginia, where the title of the col-

[67] *Ibid.*, pp. 74, 75–76.

[68] *Journals of Virginia House of Burgesses,* 1758–61, pp. 281–82.

[69] *Ibid.*, 1758–61, pp. 283, 289.

[70] *Ibid.*, C. O. 5. 1329, letter of Governor Fauquier to B. T., March
13, 1760.

ony was free of rival claims, and by 1760 applications were being made for land patents. He refused to make any grants until he had instructions from the Crown.[71]

The course followed by Fauquier and the Crown's military officers was ultimately to receive official sanction in Great Britain. The Board of Trade in a report June 1, 1759, pointed out that the difficulties with the Indians were due chiefly to the frauds and abuses in the purchase of land, but no specific recommendations were made for doing away with the evil.[72] The next year Halifax, president of the Board, favored a proposed settlement near Lake Champlain provided it could be made and faith kept with the Indians.[73] The Board's policy, maintained until 1761, did not go beyond protection of the Indians in the possession of their land against too eager settlers.[74] Under Halifax the Board showed no inclination toward checking western settlement.

The next development in western policy came under the Earl of Egremont, successor to Pitt as secretary of state. The foreign situation promised trouble, as the Family Compact was threatening to add Spain to England's enemies. Colonial defense necessitated the winning of the Indians' friendship so that the colonies could have a quiet western frontier. The Board of Trade, probably at the instigation of Egremont, on November

[71] *Journals of Virginia House of Burgesses, 1758–61*, pp. 290, 295.

[72] *Doc. Hist. of New York*, II, 772–80; Alvord, *Mississippi Valley in British Politics*, I, 122–23.

[73] *New York Colonial Documents*, VII, 428–29, 437; Alvord, *Mississippi Valley in British Politics*, I, 123.

[74] Alvord, *Mississippi Valley in British Politics*, I, 234.

11, 1761, formed a new policy in a report on the settlement of Mohawk Valley lands. Attention was called to the danger of granting lands and settling colonies in regions where Indian claims had not been fully ascertained; the discontinuance of western settlement was recommended "until the event of the war is determined and such measures taken thereupon, with respect to our Indian allies, as shall be thought expedient." The Board's report was confirmed by the Privy Council and broadened into a general policy.[75] Thus the Easton principle, followed by Crown officers in America from 1759 through 1761, was accepted as a part of the government's program. In December, 1761, at the Crown's order, instructions regarding Indian land were sent to the governors of the royal colonies, where waste lands belonged to the king. These orders forbade the governors and commanders-in-chief in America "to pass any grant or grants to any person whatever to the territories possessed or occupied by the said Indians or the property possession of which has at any time been reserved to or claimed by them."[76] In the future people who wished to patent lands west of the Alleghanies were to apply to the governor, who should transmit the application to the Board of Trade, upon whose report the Crown would act.[77]

[75] *New York Colonial Documents*, VII, 472–76; Alvord, *Mississippi Valley in British Politics*, I, 124–26.

[76] *New York Colonial Documents*, VII, 478; Alvord, *Mississippi Valley in British Politics*, I, 126.

[77] *New York Colonial Documents*, VII, 479; Alvord, *Mississippi Valley in British Politics*, I, 126.

The power to dispose of royal lands west of the Alleghanies was thus placed directly in the Crown. If Indian rights to the land were rigidly observed, a cause of Indian hostility would be removed, and through friendly Indians additional security given the border at a time when a new enemy was about to enter the war. Defense purposes in large measure governed the issuing of the decree of 1761. The Crown's act established a course of conduct only until the end of the war, when a permanent policy could be adopted, and was one of a series that cut straight across the hopes of the land companies and individuals expecting to realize immediately on the exploitation of the West.

The Crown's orders prevented the Virginia people engaged in land speculations from continuing their operations. The land companies were balked, individuals clamoring for land promised them by Dinwiddie's proclamation for service in the campaign of 1754 had their hopes dashed, and all other persons, whether actively engaged in land speculation or not, who believed in the colony's exploitation of the West were disappointed.

The strength of these factions is largely a matter of conjecture, and their influence on Virginia's part in the last years of the war difficult to evaluate. Though they included in their numbers people prominent in the colony,[78] they were never able to dominate its course. Even with the Ohio area in the colony's grasp, they did not make Virginia keep her forces in the West after 1760, when pressure from the Cherokees developed in the

[78] Lists of land grants in *Virginia Magazine of History and Biography*, V, 175 ff., 241 ff.

Southwest. The land factions were urging support of a policy in which the colony as a whole was not interested. A safe frontier, not conquest of the West, moved Virginia to support the war. The activity of the land elements temporarily ceased when they realized that the West was closed to immediate exploitation. While the land motive was losing whatever power it might have had, economic conditions were progressively making the colony loath to continue expenses for a war from which the chief motive for support—outside pressure—was gone.

Virginia's finances were in bad condition, for war needs had required large issues of paper which had been made legal tender in payment of debt. The colony's paper money became the subject of a long controversy with the British merchants which grew out of the Virginia laws on the settlement of sterling debts in currency. Virginia's law of 1748, confirmed by an order in council, provided that judgments for sterling debts could be settled in currency at 25 per cent advance.[79] This arrangement was unsatisfactory to the British merchants because exchange fluctuated greatly, sometimes being as high as 40 per cent.[80] In 1755, at the instigation of the British government, Virginia modified the act of 1748, and the power of fixing the rate of exchange at which the amount could be paid in currency was placed in the hands of the judges.[81] The British merchants were not pleased with this arrangement, and their dissatisfaction

[79] *Journals of Virginia House of Burgesses*, 1761–65, p. 191.

[80] Beer, *British Colonial Policy*, p. 179.

[81] Hening, *Statutes*, VI, 478–83.

increased when Virginia began to issue paper money.[82] The amount of paper grew as the war advanced, and despite the legal-tender quality and provisions for redemption the notes steadily depreciated. In 1757 exchange was at 135, in 1759, at 140, and in 1762, at 165.[83] The courts, under the law of 1755, attempted to place the exchange at an amount which would pay the London debt without loss to the British merchant,[84] but they were not always successful. In some cases exchange had risen 5, 10, and even 15 per cent between the time of the court order and the time of obtaining a remittance.[85] The London and Bristol merchants memorialized the Board of Trade against Virginia's paper issues. The merchants also claimed that the law of 1748 could not be legally repealed by the law of 1755 until the latter was confirmed by the Crown. Consequently they ran the risk of being paid under the old law of 1748, with its 25 per cent advance, and would suffer considerable loss as the rate of exchange was above 25 per cent.[86] Glasgow merchants declared that most of the debts due to British merchants were in currency and had been contracted on the basis of the former low exchange. The action of Virginia in making her paper legal tender for debt amount-

[82] *Journals of Virginia House of Burgesses*, 1761–65, pp. 188–89.

[83] *Ripley*, Financial History of Virginia, 139–40; Beer, *British Colonial Policy*, p. 181.

[84] *Journals of Virginia House of Burgesses*, 1761–65, pp. 173–74; Hening, *Statutes*, VI, 478–79.

[85] *Journals of Virginia House of Burgesses*, 1761–65, pp. 173–74; Beer, *British Colonial Policy*, pp. 181–82.

[86] *Journals of Virginia House of Burgesses*, 1758–61, pp. 40–41; 1761–65, p. 191; Beer, *British Colonial Policy*, pp. 181–82.

ed to a partial repudiation of her people's obligations, although the colony was innocent of any such purpose. The British merchant was naturally indignant at what was practically a scaling down of the debt due him, and objected to the legal-tender quality of the paper.[87]

The repeated complaints of the British merchants made Great Britain act to prevent such evils in the future. In 1751 Parliament had passed an act regulating the issue of paper money. The measure was one of censure, and the colonies that had not offended were not included in it. After its experience with Virginia, Parliament in 1764 forbade the issue of legal tender paper in all the colonies. The measure caused some hardship for the colonists and was a factor in the later separation from Great Britain.

The complaints of the merchants were first heard in Virginia in November, 1759, when Governor Fauquier advised the burgesses to make the debts due British merchants payable in sterling.[88] The house resolved that the merchants were secure in the recovery of their sterling debts, and refused to do anything further.[89] Fauquier was unable to push his views on the burgesses because he was dependent upon paper money for the support of the regiment. The first issues of paper were due to be retired in 1759, and were promptly redeemed, but the public did not have the same trust in the issue of 1760. Their distrust became greater in 1761 because of the variety of issues and the different times of redemp-

[87] Beer, *British Colonial Policy*, 181–82.
[88] *Journals of Virginia House of Burgesses*, 1758–61, p. 134.
[89] *Ibid.*, 1758–61, p. 141.

tion. The assembly, to allay all suspicion, made all the notes in circulation redeemable in 1769.[90]

In November, 1762, Governor Fauquier again called the burgesses' attention to the scarcity of gold and silver and advised them to act only after due deliberation because there was danger in meddling with "mediums of Trade and Commerce."[91] He also asked for the continuance of the regiment. The governor was unfortunate in introducing the paper-money question with that of furnishing troops. It will be remembered that pressure on the colony from the enemy had practically ceased. No longer influenced by the needs of defense, the burgesses permitted the paper-money controversy to dominate their attitude toward continuing the regiment. They explained that the treasury notes had caused complaints, particularly from the merchants of Great Britain, and a new issue which would be necessary to continue the regiment would only increase the complaints. They argued further that another issue of notes would depreciate earlier issues and injure the colony's trade. For these reasons they refused to continue the regiment beyond December 1, 1762, the date set by the March assembly of that year.[92]

The question of defense in Virginia continued through 1763 to be subordinate to that of paper money. In a session of the assembly called in May to consider the question of sterling remittances the burgesses absolutely refused to alter the legal-tender character of Vir-

[90] Hening, *Statutes*, VII, 465–66.

[91] *Journals of Virginia House of Burgesses*, 1761–65, p. 65.

[92] *Ibid.*, 1761–65, p. 15.

ginia's paper.[93] They could only be persuaded to appoint a committee to examine the security of the notes. The committee reported that the taxes for securing them would produce by October, 1769, over £11,000 more than the value of notes in circulation.[94] The assembly then attempted to increase confidence in the treasury notes by requiring the treasurer to give notice from time to time of the amount of paper in circulation after March 1, 1765, and to call in and destroy all notes which would no longer pass current after that date.[95]

After this statement and bolstering up of the colony's currency the burgesses defended their course, declaring that they were but following the example of the other colonies in supplying the lack of specie by paper. They continued:

Even then we chose at first to borrow £10,000 . . . . at the high interest of six per Centum, and never till after that Resource failed went into a Measure so little relished . . . . there were no warm Advocates for Paper Money among us, further than to preserve the Credit of what hath been issued, and to prevent the evil consequences of stopping its Circulation at this Time. , . . . The Want of Specie . . . . was the sole Cause of issuing our Notes, there will require no other Reason to be assigned for our not circulating them upon the Footing of Bank of Exchequer Notes.[96]

In their justification the burgesses claimed that the merchants had no cause for complaining. In the case of sterling debts the court always had fixed the rate of exchange fairly. They considered the law of 1755 valid, though it had not received the royal approbation, and if

[93] Ibid., 1761–65, pp. 171–72, 173–74.   [95] Ibid., 1761–65, p.181.

[94] Ibid., 1761–65, p. 177.   [96] Ibid., 1761–65, pp. 188–90.

the merchants thought otherwise they should not present petitions, but should get that act confirmed by the Crown.[97]

The paper-money question completely dominated the assembly during 1763 and 1764 and prevented aid from Virginia in subduing Pontiac's rebellion. The Treaty of Paris, 1763, ended all danger from Spain and France. British regulars still in America were free for use against the Indians and were holding the Ohio posts. Virginia felt her militia was sufficient to protect her border, and Governor Fauquier, knowing his assembly's temper, made no effort to have Virginia furnish troops to act with the British forces.[98] He made no request for troops until January, 1764, when he requested five hundred men for the southern district, but the house refused because the grant would require more paper.[99] During 1763 and 1764 Virginia's only assistance to the British forces defending her border was her militia.[100] In December, while the assembly was still in session, Bouquet's peace of November 17, 1764, with the Ohio Indians was laid before the house, which at once asked the governor to disband the militia.[101] The burgesses wanted to cut down all expenses possible and thus lessen the burden of high taxes. Bouquet's peace and the assembly's requests that the colony be put on a peace basis ended the 14-year struggle with the French and Indians for the trans-Alleghany country.

[97] *Ibid.*, 1761–65, pp. 188–92.   [98] *Ibid.*, 1761–65, pp. 202, 203.

[99] *Ibid.*, 1761–65, pp. 203–4, 212.

[100] *Ibid.*, 1761–65, pp. 203–4, 206–7, 212, 222, 228.

[101] *Ibid.*, 1761–65, pp. 289, 290, 291.

BIBLIOGRAPHY

MANUSCRIPT SOURCES

A wide variety of manuscript data exists for the research student fortunate enough to visit the Public Record Office in London. The Sessional Papers and Acts give a fairly comprehensive idea of the relations between the colonial governors and their assemblies, the attitude of the people to the French and Indian War, and general colonial activities. The correspondence of important colonials to government bureaus, rich in content and personality, renders the picture more complete.

VIRGINIA

Original Correspondence, Board of Trade, C. O. 5. 1327–30, 1366, 1367 (1748–64).

Original Correspondence, Secretary of State, C. O. 5. 1338, 1344, 1345 (1726–83).

Council Journals, C. O. 5. 1423, 1429, 1435 (1737–68).

Entry Books, etc., C. O. 5. 1366–68 (1728–68).

NORTH CAROLINA

Original Correspondence, Board of Trade, C. O. 5. 297–99 (1750–66).

Original Correspondence, Secretary of State, C. O. 5. 307–10 (1749–83).

Entry Books, etc., C. O. 5. 323–25 (1730–70).

SOUTH CAROLINA

Original Correspondence, Board of Trade, C. O. 5. 371–77 (1745–64).

Original Correspondence, Secretary of State, C. O. 5. 385–99 (1744–67).

Acts, C. O. 5. 419–22 (1746–66).

Sessional Papers, C. O. 5. 460–83 (1749–65).

Entry Books, etc., C. O. 5. 402–4 (1739–74).

MARYLAND

Original Correspondence, Secretary of State, C. O. 5. 721 (1704–80).

PENNSYLVANIA

Original Correspondence, Secretary of State, C. O. 5. 1233 (1690–1767).

PROPRIETARIES

Original Correspondence, Board of Trade, C. O. 5. 1274–76 (1754–64); 1280 (1762–67).

AMERICA AND WEST INDIES

Original Documents, C. O. 5. 6–7 (1749–79).

PRINTED SOURCES

A. GENERAL COLLECTIONS

The best printed sources for an adequate idea of Virginia during this period can be found in the proceedings of its representative body, the *Journals of the House of Burgesses of Virginia,* 1659, 1660–76, edited by H. R. McIlwaine and J. P. Kennedy, 12 vols. (Richmond, 1905–15). The account given here of political, social, and economic conditions is well supplemented by the laws found in W. W. Hening, *The Statutes at Large, Being a Collection of all the Laws of Virginia,* 1619–1792, 13 vols. (Philadelphia and New York, 1823). Of little value other than as a check against the *Journals of the House of Burgesses of Virginia* are the *Legislative Journals of the Council of Colonial Virginia,* edited by H. R. McIlwaine, 3 vols. (Richmond, 1918–19).

Similar material showing the reaction of the people of Pennsylvania toward the conflict is given in *Minutes of the Provincial Council of Pennsylvania, 1683–1776,* 10 vols. (Harrisburg, 1851–52), "Pennsylvania Colonial Records." This series reflects the point of view of the executive, shows his relations with the house, and contains valuable data concerning the frontier and Indian situation. *Votes and Proceedings of the House of Representatives of the Province of Pennsylvania, 1682–1776,* 6 vols. (Philadelphia, 1752–76), also give the relations of governor and house, but from the angle of the house. *Pennsylvania Archives, 1st series*, edited by Samuel Hazard, 12 vols. (Philadelphia, 1852–56), is a compilation of documents throwing some light on the economic and social life of the people and supplementing the material of the executive and legislative records.

Corresponding to the Virginia and Pennsylvania collections are the *Colonial Records of North Carolina*, edited by W. L. Saunders, vols. I–X, XXIII–XXV (Raleigh, 1886–90), which contain an unusually complete account of the relations between governor and assembly and the support given to the war by the colony.

Other general sources which do not bear directly on this study but furnish some facts regarding the land situation in Virginia are *Documents Relative to the Colonial History of the State of New York*, edited by E. B. O'Callaghan, 11 vols. (Albany, 1856–60; E. B. O'Callaghan, *The Documentary History of the State of New York*, 4 vols. (Albany, 1850–51); *Calendar of Virginia State Papers*, edited by W. Palmer, 7 vols. (Richmond, 1875–83).

B. CORRESPONDENCE, WRITINGS, AND SPECIAL MATERIAL

Considerable data on the land question, the Indian trade, the military operations, and conditions on the frontier can be gleaned from *The Official Records of Robert Dinwiddie, Lieutenant-Governor of Virginia, 1751–58*, edited by R. A. Brock, 2 vols. (Richmond, 1883–84), which is also valuable for its details regarding the relations between governor and assembly; and *Correspondence of Horatio Sharpe*, edited by W. H. Browne, 3 vols. (Baltimore, 1888, 1890, 1895), *Maryland Archives*, Vols. VI, IX, XIV, likewise portraying relations between governor and assembly and contacts of the former with the proprietor.

Correspondence of William Pitt When Secretary of State with Colonial Governors and Military and Naval Commanders in America, edited by G. S. Kimball, 2 vols. (New York, 1906), relates sufficiently military operations from 1758 to 1760 and contains information concerning grants made by the colonies to the service.

Wraxall's Abridgement of the New York Indian Records, edited by C. H. McIlwain (Cambridge, 1915), not only specializes on Indian relations in the colony of New York, but also furnishes a fairly good portrayal of the Indian trade on the whole western frontier. Further information concerning Indian relations in the West is found in *Journal of Christopher Gist*, edited by W. M. Darlington (Pittsburgh, 1893); "New Trading Posts To Be Established in the West, Extract from a letter of the Directors of the Company of the Colony of Canada," in *Collections of the State Historical Society of Wisconsin*, edited by R. G. Thwaites, 20 vols. (Madison, 1855–1915), XVI, 208–10; "Observations on the late and present Conduct of the French with Regard to Their Encroachments upon the British Colonies in North America, Together with Remarks on the Importance of These Colonies to Great Britain," in the *Magazine of History*, Extra Numbers, XVI; J. S. Bassett, *The Writings of "Colonel William Byrd of Westover in Virginia, Esquire"* (New York, 1901).

The work of most value regarding land colonization before the French and Indian War is *Benjamin Franklin's Writings*, edited by A. H. Smyth, 10 vols. (New York, 1905). After that time the land question is best portrayed in *Letters to Washington and Accompanying Papers*, edited by S. M. Hamilton, 5 vols. (Boston and New York, 1898); and *The Writings of George Washington*, edited by W. C. Ford, 14 vols. (New York, 1889), which also give fragmentary information concerning military conditions on the western frontier. "Draper Manuscripts," in *Journals of the House of Burgesses of Virginia*, 1758–61, appendix (Richmond, 1908) and "Bancroft Transcripts," in *Journals of the House of Burgesses of Virginia*, 1758–61, appendix (Richmond, 1908) describe speculation in western lands and military operations on the southwestern frontier. *Report on Canadian Archives*, edited by Douglas Brymner (Ottawa, 1890), treats of the land situation after 1758 and the story of the Forbes Expedition. *The Preston and Virginia Papers of the Draper Collection of Manuscripts, Publications of the State Historical Society of Wisconsin* (Madison, 1915), depict conditions of land settlement and life of the frontier population. A further description of frontier conditions can be found in Andrew Burnaby, *Travels through the Middle Settlements in North America in the Years of 1759 and 1760* (London, 1775), and A. S. Withers, *Chronicles of Border Warfare, or a History of the Set-*

tlement, by the Whites, of Northwestern Virginia, edited by R. G. Thwaites (Cincinnati, 1895).

SECONDARY MATERIAL

A. GENERAL ACCOUNTS

There is no good secondary account of Virginia in this period. Some scattered facts about the colony may be secured from John Burke (Daly), *History of Virginia from Its First Settlement to the Present Day*, 3 vols. (Petersburg, 1804–5); Charles Campbell, *History of the Colony and Ancient Dominion of Virginia* (Philadelphia, 1860); J. A. C. Chandler, *Colonial Virginia* (Richmond, 1907).

Maryland conditions for these years are portrayed, but superficially, in N. D. Mereness, *Maryland as a Proprietory Province* (New York, 1901); Lady Edgar, *A Colonial Governor in Maryland, Horatio Sharpe and His Times, 1753–73* (London, 1912), and J. T. Scharf, *History of Maryland*, 3 vols. (Baltimore, 1879).

While the histories of North and South Carolina and Pennsylvania are also incomplete for these years, some material can be found in S. A. Ashe, *History of North Carolina* (Greensboro, 1908); Edward McCrady, *The History of South Carolina under Royal Government, 1719–76* (New York, 1889); Isaac Sharpless, *History of Quaker Government in Pennsylvania*, 2 vols. (Philadelphia, 1898–99).

British colonial policy is well and fully discussed in G. L. Beer, *British Colonial Policy, 1754–65* (New York, 1907), and in Thomas Pownal, *Administration of the Colonies*, 2 vols. (London, 1774).

The military movements of the war may be found in Justin Winsor, *The Mississippi Basin: The Struggle in America between England and France, 1697–1763* (Boston, 1895).

B. SPECIAL ACCOUNTS

British policy toward western land is ably described in C. W. Alvord, *The Mississippi Valley in British Politics*, 2 vols. (Cleveland, 1917).

Accounts of the Ohio Company are given by N. B. Craig, "The Ohio Company," in the *Olden Time Magazine*, 2 vols. (Pittsburgh, 1846–48), I, 291 ff.; Berthold Fernow, *The Ohio Valley in Colonial Days* (Albany, New York, 1890); and H. T. Leyland, "The Ohio Company," in *Quarterly Publication of the Historical and Philosophical Society of Ohio*, XVI, 13–14. The movements of the people west are best described in F. J. Turner, *The Frontier in American History* (New York, 1920); C. E. Kemper, "Early Westward Movement in Virginia," in *Virginia Magazine of History and Biography*, Vols. XII, XIII; Samuel Kercheval, *A History of the Valley of Virginia* (Winchester, 1833). Fragments on this same subject may be found in J. P. Arthur, *Western North Carolina, 1730–1913* (Raleigh, 1914); C. H. Ambler, *Sectionalism in Virginia* (Chicago, 1910); Bolivar Christian, *The Scotch-Irish Settlers in the Valley of Virginia* (Richmond, 1860); O. F. Morton, *A History of Highland County, Virginia* (1911) and *A History of Rockbridge County, Virginia* (Staunton, 1920); William C. Pendleton, *History of Tazewell County and Southwest Virginia, 1748–1920* (Richmond, 1920); L. P. Summers, *History of Southwest Virginia* (Richmond, 1903); J. W. Wayland, *A History of Rockingham County, Virginia* (Dayton, 1912); and *The German Element of the Shenandoah Valley of Virginia* (Charlottesville, 1907).

The composition and proceedings of the legislature of Virginia are described in detail by J. A. C. Chandler, "Representation in Virginia," in *Johns Hopkins University Studies*, Vol. XIX, Nos. 6, 7 (Baltimore, 1896); A. E. McKinley, *Suffrage Franchise in the English Colonies* (New York, 1905); E. I. Miller, "The Legislature of the Province of Virginia, Its Internal Development," in *Columbia University Studies*, Vol. XXVIII, No. 2 (New York, 1917). The administrative organization of Virginia is given by P. S. Flippin, *The Royal Government in Virginia, 1624–1775* (New York, 1919). An excellent account of the relations of the British government with Pennsylvania is contained in W. T. Root, *The Relations of Pennsylvania with the British Government, 1696–1765* (New York, 1912); and some material bearing on North

Carolina's relations to the Crown may be found in C. F. Raper, *North Carolina: A Study in English Colonial Government* (New York, 1904).

The Indian situation in the West and the traders' activities are fully related by C. A. Hanna, *The Wilderness Trail*, 2 vols. (New York, 1911).

Some material on the finances of Virginia and North Carolina may be found in C. J. Bullock, *The Monetary History of the United States* (New York, 1900), and in W. Z. Ripley, *The Financial History of Virginia* (New York, 1893).

COLLECTIONS OF PERIODICALS

The most important periodical containing data regarding the western history of Virginia for this period is the *Virginia Magazine of History and Biography* (Richmond, 1893——). The reprints of documents in this magazine constitute a mine of information for the student. There is also much valuable material in the *William and Mary College Quarterly Historical Magazine* (Williamsburg, 1892–1919, 1921——).

For the other colonies the best periodicals are the *Maryland Historical Magazine* (Baltimore, 1906——); the *Pennsylvania Magazine of History and Biography* (Philadelphia, 1877——), and the *South Carolina Historical and Genealogical Magazine* (Charleston, 1900——).

INDEX